The Employment Effect of
Technical Change

The Employment Effect of Technical Change

A Theoretical Study of New Technology and the Labour Market

Y.S. Katsoulacos
Lecturer in Economics
University of Bristol

Wheatsheaf
Books

DISTRIBUTED BY HARVESTER PRESS

First published in Great Britain in 1986 by
WHEATSHEAF BOOKS LTD
A MEMBER OF THE HARVESTER PRESS PUBLISHING GROUP
Publisher: John Spiers
Director of Publications: Edward Elgar
16 Ship Street, Brighton, Sussex

©Y.S. Katsoulacos, 1986

British Library Cataloguing in Publication Data
Katsoulacos, Y.S.
  Technical change and the labour market: a theoretical
  study of the employment effect of product and process
  innovation.
  1. Labor supply—Effect of technological innovation
  I. Title
  331.12′5   HD6331
  ISBN 0–7450–0133–5

Typeset in 11 point Times Roman
by Photo·Graphics, Honiton, Devon
Printed in Great Britain by Oxford University Press

THE HARVESTER PRESS PUBLISHING GROUP
The Harvester Press Publishing Group comprises Harvester Press
Limited (chiefly publishing literature, fiction, philosophy,
psychology, and science and trade books), Harvester Press
Microform Publications Limited (publishing in microform
unpublished archives, scarce printed sources, and indexes to these
collections) and Wheatsheaf Books Limited (a wholly independent
company chiefly publishing in economics, international politics,
sociology and related social sciences), whose books are distributed
by The Harvester Press Limited and its agencies throughout the
world.

To my Mother and Father

Contents

vii

B: Product Innovation

PART TWO: THE EFFECT OF INNOVATION IN THE LONG RUN

Foreword

This study of technical change and employment is a truly original and remarkable book, for several reasons. It is an important landmark in the development of economic theory in a hitherto neglected area, but one which is of the greatest contemporary significance. It has profound implications, not merely for theory, but for economic and employment policy in all industrialised countries.

The debate with which the book is concerned goes back to Ricardo's famous remark in the third edition of his *Principles of Political Economy* that:

The opinion entertained by the labouring class, that the employment of machinery is frequently detrimental to their interests, is not founded on prejudice and error, but is conformable to the correct principles of political economy.

As the author points out, mainstream classical and neo-classical analysis has hitherto paid scant attention to *product* innovation, and has focused almost exclusively on *process* innovation. This one-sided emphasis has also spilled over into the wider more popular debate. Good examples are the automation debate of the 1950s and the more recent controversies over the employment effects of micro-electronics.

Dr. Katsoulacos shows convincingly that, even within the assumptions of neo-classical equilibrium analysis, the employment effects of *product* innovations (and this includes of course new services) are quite different and far more positive over a relatively short period, than those of process innovations.

This demonstration is extraordinarily important since it provides a firm foundation, even within that conventional theory which supposedly governs much economic analysis and policy-making in the Western world, for conclusions which have also emerged from some of the best recent empirical research on technical change and employment. The studies, for example, of Eliasson and his colleagues in Sweden, of PROGNOS in Germany or of Kuwahara in Japan, indicate clearly that those countries which are able to gain technological leadership in the production (and export) of new capital goods, consumer goods, components and services may enjoy very favourable direct and even greater indirect employment benefits. Those economies, on the other hand, which are relatively passive recipients of imported process technology and the associated equipment may experience prolonged problems of structural unemployment during major technological revolutions, such as that associated with information technology.

Our own empirical work on technical change and employment at the Science Policy Research Unit (the 'TEMPO' project) points strongly in the same direction, although contained within a somewhat different theoretical framework, as described by Dr. Katsoulacos.

This means, to coin a phrase, not only that the opinions of the 'labouring class' about process innovations, are not necessarily founded on 'prejudice and error', but also that the opinions of many technologists about the importance of policies designed to promote the development of new products and services within the national economy, may conform 'to the correct principles of political economy'. Policy implications are not the concern of this book, but I believe nevertheless that the need for economic policy, and especially for employment policy, to take on board an explicit technological dimension, has never been more clearly and logically demonstrated.

Christopher Freeman
Science Policy Research Unit
University of Sussex
March 1985

Preface

The present book is intended as a contribution to the *economic analysis* of the employment effects of technical change. The preoccupation with economic analysis is not the result of a belief that 'economics' or the 'analytical method' are always the appropriate vehicles to use for enhancing our understanding of the complex processes through which technical change may act on the labour market. Rather, it reflects the view that, despite the long-standing interest of economists on the possible effects of technological progress, little has been done to investigate the question within the framework of economic theory.

The book also offers a survey of existing work in the area of technical change and its effects on employment. This is, I believe, quite complete as far as the non-empirical work is concerned. Nevertheless, and because no *new* empirical evidence has been generated here, an attempt has been made throughout the book to relate results to available empirical evidence. There is now a quite extensive empirical literature to which the reader is referred whenever appropriate.

The book is divided into two parts dealing with the short run and long run respectively. Part One is subdivided into Section A, dealing with process innovation, and Section B, dealing with product innovation. In Section A I first review the existing (partial equilibrium) theoretical work on the short-run effect of process innovation; I then generalise this work by extending it to the case of imperfectly competitive markets. A general equilibrium model is then developed (in Chapter 3) to examine the effect on aggregate labour demand and supply of general and sector-specific process innovation. Section B starts with a review of existing ideas and uses a simple model to obtain some preliminary results on the relation between product innovation and employment (Chapter 4). In Chapter 5 I use the recently developed 'Natural Oligopoly' model to re-examine and reject the intuitively plausible notion that product innovation may not affect employment if it involves the replacement of an existing consumer good by a new improved variety. The impact (or short-run) effect on employment of product innovation is positive, whilst that of process innovation may be negative. Thus I provide theoretical foundations for the often quoted empirical observation that product innovation 'is more likely to have a favourable employment effect'.

In Part Two, which deals with process innovation only, the emphasis shifts to the long run. I examine the capital accumulation process induced by process innovation first under the assumption that prices are flexible and then for a fixprice economy. In the first case we get convergence to a new Walrasian equilibrium. In the second we find that the long-run equilibrium may exhibit dynamic instability in the sense that the transition path does not converge to long-run equilibrium but involves ever-increasing unemployment. This part also deals with aspects of technical change repercussions that arise in connection with the capital formation process and with structural unemployment.

The book is a revised version of my Ph.D. thesis submitted and approved in the summer of 1984 at the London School of Economics. I would like to take this opportunity to express my sincere gratitude to my thesis supervisor, Dr J. Sutton, for his constant encouragement, help, and advice, which enabled me to complete the thesis. I would also like to thank P. Stoneman, who in his capacity as external examiner, made many helpful comments and suggestions.

February 1985

1 Introduction

1.1 INTRODUCTORY REMARKS

The past decade has seen a significant renewal of concern with the effect of technological progress on employment.[1] Economists' traditional preoccupation with the subject can be traced back to Ricardo's inclusion of the chapter on 'Machinery' in the third edition of his *Principles of Political Economy*.

The present book develops some new analytical results on the effects of technical change on the labour market. In most cases I start from a state of equilibrium and ask: how is the labour market affected by the introduction of an innovation? I seek an answer to this question under a variety of circumstances concerning the type of innovation, the time period under consideration and market structure. The existing theoretical literature on the subject is incomplete to the extent that it has concentrated on the employment effects of process innovation, in the short run,[2] in perfectly competitive product markets.

Technical change may be broadly divided into process and product innovation. By the latter I mean the introduction of a new consumer good, by the former any change that enables firms to produce their current outputs at reduced cost. Process innovation may be subdivided into disembodied and embodied; the former expressing an increase in efficiency of the firm's existing inputs, the latter being a change that is embodied in new capital goods. Whilst below

1

I will, on occasion, find it useful to introduce explicitly the notion of embodied technical change—in dealing with the long-term effects of technical change and/or its effect during the transition path between Walrasian equilibria—it is the product–process division that is most relevant to the discussion.

As we shall see below, the distinction between product and process innovation is prominent in much of the recent empirical literature and public discussions on the employment effects of technical change. It has, in particular, been repeatedly suggested—though no theoretical justification has been provided for this suggestion—that product innovation, unlike process innovation, has 'job-creating' effects: to quote from a recent contribution to this argument 'if in the future labour-saving process innovations grew significantly relative to product innovations, the dangers of serious unemployment of new entrants to the labour market, and of older workers displaced by technical change, would increase'.[3] One of my main tasks below will be to examine the extent to which theoretical foundations may be provided for this argument. To accomplish this task I will have to examine, for the first time, the general equilibrium effects of product innovations.

1.2 STRANDS IN THE LITERATURE ON THE EMPLOYMENT EFFECT OF TECHNICAL CHANGE

One may distinguish three strands in the existing literature that is concerned with the relation between employment and technical change:

1. Theoretical studies have examined the effect of technical change on employment, labour being treated as a homogeneous factor of production. These have dealt exclusively with process innovation and have been mainly concerned with deriving the conditions sufficient to ensure that such innovation reduces labour demand at given wages.

This tradition starts with the publication of the third edition of Ricardo's *Principles* that included, for the first time, the famous 'Machinery' chapter. Subsequent comments on the subject were very sparse. In a short survey, written in 1932, Kaldor considered the most 'comprehensive *modern* statement' on the subject to be Nicholson's *The Effect of the Introduction of Machinery on Wages*, London, 1892, and noted that 'this puts more emphasis on questions of institutional environment than on analytical problems'.[4] Renewed interest followed the high unemployment of the 1920s and 1930s. Several articles and books appeared in the early 1930s, followed (in 1940) by a comprehensive 'survey' of the literature on technological unemployment by Gourvitch.[5]

More recently, Hicks' *Capital and Time* (1973), examined the transition path between steady states of an economy, following the introduction of an innovation. Hicks' analysis was developed in a growth theoretic framework. As I show below, a model similar to that of Hicks provides a useful vehicle within which to examine the effect on the equilibrium level of employment of process innovation in the long run. Finally, we must include two recent articles by Neary (1981) and by Sinclair (1981) in which a precise statement is given of the conditions under which technical change will reduce labour demand in the short run, in a competitive industry.

As far as product innovation is concerned, there has been no analysis of its impact on the aggregate employment level. As a recent author puts it, 'nearly all the discussion refers to changes in process technology. Modelling the impact of changes in product technology at the macro-level is an area that is much less analysed—not because of its irrelevance but because of its difficulty'.[6]

2. A second group of studies—mostly of a purely empirical character—have been concerned with the effect of technical change on the skill composition of the labour force. Much of the literature on the relation between

employment and technical change, over the last three decades or so, has been preoccupied with this issue, concentrating on the apparent influence of technological progress in raising the demand for skilled relative to unskilled workers and the extent to which observed unemployment levels have a high structural component. The 'structural unemployment thesis' that gained prominence in the USA in the first part of the 1960s argued that much of the rising unemployment in the western industrialised world was due to a decline in opportunities for the unskilled group of workers due to technological progress. This thesis, which has made a reappearance in recent years, has never been examined formally. Below I develop a simple model to investigate the conditions under which the structuralist thesis will hold.

3. Finally, there are a number of studies concerned with the relation between technical change and long-term *variations* in employment and output—both at the sectoral level, and for the economy as a whole. Here the most distinguishing characteristic of what may be termed the Schumpeterian approach to long-wave theory is the emphasis on the role of technical change in explaining fluctuations in economic activity over long periods.

To explain long-run cyclical movements in market economies, these studies argue that the introduction of innovations is not a smooth process occurring at a more or less constant rate with similar effect on all the sectors of the economy. Instead, it is argued, technical change is 'extremely uneven over *time*; as between *industries* and broad sectors of the economy; and *geographically* as between regions and countries'. At times of diffusion 'of clusters of technical innovations of wide adaptability' there are created 'many new opportunities for investment and employment' that lead to a 'substantial upthrust to the growth of the economic system'. As the diffusion process comes to an end, and before a new cluster gets under way, several factors—such as 'standardisation, economies of scale and cost-reducing technical change'—interact to 'reduce the employment generated per unit of investment', this being an 'important part in the cyclical movement from boom to recession'.[7] The relation between the product–process innovation distinction and this (neo-Schumpeterian) long-wave theory, is that the latter may be easily interpreted as associating the expansionary investment of long-term upswings with the introduction of new consumer goods, with process innovation mainly occurring in the movement from boom to recession and in the recession period itself.[8]

Throughout the present analysis, I will follow for the most part the first of these three strands. One chapter, however, will be devoted to structural unemployment, and the overall thrust of the present study may be interpreted as an attempt to formalise certain of the ideas used in neo-Schumpeterian long-wave theory. Nonetheless, it may avoid some potential ambiguities to remark here that when I refer below to 'the economic analysis of the employment effect of technical change' I have in mind (unless otherwise stated) the work associated with this first strand of the literature, being the strand which has dominated discussion of these issues among economic theorists.

A detailed review of the contents of the book is given in section 1.4.

1.3   SOME NOTES ON PREVIOUS THEORETICAL WORK AND ON METHODOLOGY

In contrast to the more recent literature, theoretical discussions of the interwar period on the employment effects of technical change took for granted the use of equilibrium theory. As a consequence, it was often suggested that the main issue for investigation concerned the effects of technical change on distributive shares, rather than involuntary unemployment. It was argued that the effect of technical change on labour's share is likely to be favourable—even when the initial, that is, short-run, effect is not. All this is clear from the following remarks from the early work of Kaldor and Hicks, which also provide a useful background for much of the later discussions.

In an attempt to justify the fact that 'hardly any monographic comprehensive investigation has been undertaken' on the relation between technical change and employment, Kaldor, in his 1932 survey, pointed to two facts.

Firstly, the optimistic conclusions regarding the effects of inventions follow self-evidently from the general notions of the theory of equilibrium and, therefore, do not seem to demand a special proof. Secondly, as the trend of events during the latter part of the nineteenth century seemed to support the views of the economists—a great expansion in the use of machinery went hand in hand with a rise in population and a rise in real wages—the generally accepted view [that rejects 'the popular claim that inventions tend to diminish the volume of employment and lower the wages of workers'] was never seriously challenged. ...

Kaldor continues by pointing to the changed situation following the first World War:

Far reaching technical changes were introduced which even prompted some people to announce the advent of a 'second industrial revolution'. Unemployment appeared on a grand scale *pari passu* with these industrial changes, and showed little tendency to diminish. ... It was only natural that these two things should be linked together in the public mind and that the pessimistic views about the effects of the introduction of machinery on labour, so familiar in the early days of the industrial revolution, should make their reappearance. ... Today there is scarcely any political or journalistic observer of world affairs who does not attribute to the rapid growth of technical improvements one of the major causes of the present trouble.[9]

What is noteworthy, in the present context, is the fact that Kaldor is here reviewing a book on technological unemployment; he criticises its author for not 'confining his analysis to clearing up under what conditions technical progress will have harmful effects on the share of labour in the national dividend' but attempting to 'single out technical progress ... [making] it responsible ... [implicitly assuming that anything that diminishes the share of labour in the notional dividend will cause lasting unemployment], for a state of disequilibrium which may become cumulative'.[10]

Note that above Kaldor relies on 'equilibrium theory' to argue that technical change will have a favourable effect on labour's share. It is worthwhile pursuing this point further by introducing Hicks' comments on the subject in his *Theory of Wages*. As Hicks writes:

A labour-saving invention ... need not actually diminish the marginal product of labour, and consequently labour's absolute share in the dividend; it may do so if it is very labour-saving: ...

Some inventions of this kind doubtless occur fairly frequently, but if they are—as is probably usual—merely a small part of general inventive activity, then it is most unlikely that their influence will be dominant. For if they tend to reduce labour's marginal product, there are simultaneously at work other forces, derived from the increase of capital and the expansion of autonomous invention, tending to increase the marginal product of labour. There can be no doubt that these latter forces are usually far more powerful. ...

Thus, so far as the absolute share of labour is concerned, ... it is possible but extremely improbable that economic progress may cause a decline in the equilibrium level of real wages. And further, it should be remembered, even if this unlikely event should materialise, it would be temporary; enlarged profits would mean new savings; increased capital would raise the level of real wages again.[11]

Commenting on the same subject much more recently, Hicks repeats—perhaps more clearly—the above argument. Thus, in *Economic Perspectives* (1977), he writes:

A technical change, if it is to be profitable, must raise the marginal product of at least one factor; but it does not have to raise the marginal product of both factors. Thus, as between two factors, 'labour' and 'capital', it is possible that the marginal product of each may be raised, but it is also possible that that of one factor may be diminished. Thus it is not excluded, in neoclassical terms, that a 'strongly labour-saving invention' may diminish the marginal product of labour. But if it does so, our neoclassic would say, the marginal product of capital must be increased; so profits must be increased. The increase in profits must facilitate accumulation; and an increase in capital, with no further labour saving change, must increase the marginal product of labour. So it all comes out 'for the best' in the end, just as Ricardo (in his chapter on Machinery) said. (p. 186).

Now, as noted in the previous section, it was only very recently, (in two articles published simultaneously in *Oxford Economic Papers* in 1981)[12] that the conditions under which technical change will reduce the short-run demand for labour by a competitive industry at given real wages (i.e., the conditions that make technical change 'strongly labour-saving', so that labour's marginal physical product is reduced, to use Hicks' terminology) were formally investigated. The authors also investigated the conditions under which technical change will reduce the *value* of the marginal product of labour, that is, will reduce labour demand (by a competitive industry) at given *nominal* wages. Nonetheless, the analysis has, up to now, remained mainly concerned with the short-run partial equilibrium effect on employment of process innovation in perfectly competitive markets. In the next section I summarise a number of ways in which I extend these recent contributions to the analysis of the employment effect of technical change. However, a few more remarks on the use of equilibrium theory would now be pertinent.

In contrast to the situation during the interwar period, a fundamental assumption for much of recent literature on the relation between technical change and employment—especially that on structural unemployment and long-wave theory—is that the wage rate is not perfectly flexible, at least in the downward direction (in the sense that it does not respond fast enough to equilibrate the labour market over short periods of time, when there is excess supply in this market). How does one account for wage stickiness? An extensive review of sources of wage stickiness is provided in at least two recent articles by Solow.[13] To quote from his conclusions, whilst it may be reasonable to follow orthodox theory and:

presume that agents do the best they can, subject to whatever constraints [are present] ... in some contexts the traditional formulations of the objective function and constraints may be inappropriate.

In the labour market, the participants are firms and groups of firms on one side, and individual workers, organised trade unions, and informally organised labour pools on the other. ... [If they] feel constrained, to some nontrivial degree, by social customs that have to do with the wage and wage-setting procedures, the result is that factor prices turn up in our equations in unfamiliar ways.... [To] mention a few examples ... if Keynes was right about the conventional significance of relative wages, then ratios of wage rates appear in the objective functions on the labour side. If the current or future performance of workers depends on their feelings that wage rates are fair, then wage rates appear in the production functions constraining firms. In both cases the result may be to 'preserve [in the presence of excess labour supply] the general wage level or its trend, but that is an unintended artifact'.[14]

In a recent article, Georgescu-Roegen and Fitoussi[15] advanced a novel explanation of price stickiness, which is particularly relevant to our present analysis. They argued that the continuous technical change experienced in the western world since the Second World War is the most important reason for such stickiness.They first cite evidence indicating that the pre-World War Two cyclical pattern of unemployment has turned, since then, into chronic (slowly) increasing unemployment. They then argue that 'the permanence of unemployment in this epoch is due to the continuous structural change brought about by novelties. This proposition means not that only one kind of unemployment— structural unemployment—is worth studying, but that at the source of any unemployment one finds structural change'.

To explain why prices do not adjust fast enough to eliminate unemployment, these authors then argue that this is exactly due to the 'continual structural shocks [that] require that microdecisions be adapted constantly and assure the permanence of market disequilibrium....' The rapidity of these shocks 'explain why prices and quantities do not have and cannot have an infinite speed of reaction' by producing a very 'high level of uncertainty, ... and a crushing complexity (that makes it impossible to obtain all relevant information)'. They go on to argue that even those institutional rules (such as long-term wage contracts) that lead into obstacles to adaptation 'come into being on the basis of the idea that some price rigidity would help prevent disequilibria associated with novelties'.

There are, then, two contrasting ways (fixprice or flexprice) of approaching the analysis of the employment effect of innovation. An assumption that the wage rate is not perfectly flexible will not be invoked in most of the analysis which follows. My approach, rather, will be to focus attention on the factors that determine the effect of process and product innovation on the demand and supply of labour and, hence, on labour market equilibrium. My view is that equilibrium theory is sufficient for the discussion of many interesting issues concerning the effect of innovation on the labour market. However, I shall always point out the implications of my analysis were the real or the nominal wage rate inflexible. Only in Chapter 7 do I make explicit use of the notion of a fixprice economy; while in Chapter 8, in discussing structural unemployment, I assume the existence of unemployment insurance.

1.4 A BRIEF SURVEY

As has already been indicated, my present analysis has two main themes:
  1. The first, explored in *Part One*, concerns the empirical distinction between product and process innovation. I have noted above that a major theme in the empirical literature concerns an alleged contrast between the employment effect of process and product innovation—the former being said to raise unemployment, the second—possibly—to reduce it. In unravelling this distinction, we are led to examine the *impact* effect of technical change in a series of related models.

     The effect of process innovation is examined in Section A of Part One (Chapters 2 and 3) and that of product innovation in Section B (Chapters 4 and 5).

     In Chapter 2 I offer a review and some extensions to recent partial equilibrium analysis of the short-run effect of process innovation. In 2.2 I review the conditions that must be present so that process innovation reduces the marginal product of labour; these were recently obtained by Neary (1981). In 2.3 I investigate the relation between labour demand and productivity increasing process innovation at given nominal wages. In the recent papers by Neary and Sinclair (mentioned above) this relation was examined for a perfectly competitive industry. I first review their argument and then generalise their (partial equilibrium) analysis by extending it to imperfectly competitive product markets. Finally, in section 2.4 I examine for completeness the effect of process innovation on a short-run (temporary) Keynesian equilibrium.

Much of what is interesting in regard to the economic analysis of technical change is lost by focusing on a single industry. So I go on to re-examine these questions in a *general equilibrium* framework where product markets are imperfectly competitive (in Chapter 3). I examine the effect on labour demand and supply, and hence on labour market equilibrium, of both (i) general, or balanced and (ii) sector-specific process innovation. I focus on the *impact* effect of innovation where this is understood to be the short-run impact with nominal aggregate expenditure fixed.

Moving on to the second section of Part One (Chapters 4 and 5), I develop two models within which I explore the relation between product innovation and employment.

It can be shown that whilst both process and product innovation raise the level of employment that can be attained by expansionary government policy, that is, the full employment ceiling, at each level of the wage rate:

(a) For process innovation the *impact effect* may be a reduction in the level of employment. I set out precise conditions for this.

(b) For product innovation, however, even the *impact effect* involves a rise in the level of employment. *These results provide some theoretical foundation for*

the often quoted empirical observation, mentioned in
section 1.1 above, that product innovation 'is more
likely to have a favourable employment effect' than
process innovation.

2. My second main theme, explored in *Part Two* of the
book, concerns the distinction between flexible and sticky
prices in relation to the employment effect of innovation
in the long run. My aim here is to deal with two major
limitations of the analysis of Part One, the first being
associated with the assumption of fixed nominal aggregate expenditure. In Chapters 6 and 7 I endogenise
aggregate expenditure. This is done in two contrasting
ways: I use a simplified variation of a model first employed by Hicks in *Capital and Time* (1973) first under a
flexprice (neoclassical) assumption (in Chapter 6), and
then under a fixprice (neo-Keynesian) assumption (in
Chapter 7), to examine the transition path of the economy following process innovation.

In the flexprice case we get convergence to a new full
employment Walrasian equilibrium (assuming certain
stability conditions are satisfied) *whatever* the short-run
effect of the innovation is on labour demand.

*In the fixprice case, however, not only do we get an
adverse short-run effect on labour demand, but we find
that the long-run equilibrium may exhibit dynamic instability in the sense that the transition path does not spon-
taneously converge to long-run equilibrium but involves
ever increasing unemployment.*

My secondary aim in this part is to throw some light on
the mechanisms which may lead to adverse effects on
labour demand and employment over the period of
capital accumulation induced by the innovation. That is, I
wish to study those aspects of technical change repercussions that arise in connection with the process of capital
formation. (With this in mind I work throughout Part
Two with a model which includes a capital good sector.)

Part Two ends with a discussion of structural unemployment (Chapter 8). This topic finds its natural place
here, given the long-run nature of the issues associated
with the structural effects of technical change. I examine

the conditions under which the so-called 'structuralist thesis'—according to which technical change is responsible for a growth in the demand for skilled labour and the unemployment among the unskilled-labour group of workers—will be valid.

Finally, Chapter 9 offers a summary of the main results, and some concluding remarks, though the relation to empirical work, and the policy implications of the analysis, are also discussed in each one of the chapters.

NOTES

1. In the last four years there has been an explosion in publications, the majority of which are of an informal character, on the relationship between employment and technical change. *See* Clark and Cooper (1982), Freeman *et al.* (1982), Rothwell and Zegveld (1979, 1981), Stoneman *et al.* (1984), also Blattner (1979), Standing (1983), Stoneman *et al.* (1982), Thornton and Wheelock (1980), Wiles (1983), Williams (1983a,b), Wilson and Whitley (1982), and Wragg and Robertson (1978). For more formal recent discussions *see* Heffernan (1980), Stoneman (1976), also Dobbs *et al.* (1983), Neary (1981), Sinclair (1981), Stoneman and Waterson (1984). This list does not include the substantial number of works on the effect of technical change on employment via changes in international competitiveness, which are not of direct interest to us—the present work relying throughout on the assumption of a closed economy; on this, *see* Pavit (1980), Stoneman (1976, 1983). Also, in the present work, considerations related to the process of diffusion of innovation are neglected; on this, *see* Chapter 12 of Stoneman (1983), to which I also return in Part Two. There is no consensus as to the likely effect of process innovation on employment, and empirical evidence has not helped; for example in Stoneman (1983) the author summarises the empirical evidence by arguing that 'we cannot isolate any particular direction of effect of (process innovation) on factor employment' (p. 167; *see also* p. 196). On the other hand, there seems to exist a consensus that product innovation 'is more likely to have a

positive employment effect' than process innovation; to this I return below.

2. An exception to this is Stoneman (1983) (Chapter 12, and appendix to that chapter), a work that appeared after the present one was near completion. Chapters 11 and 12 of this work are most relevant to our own concerns and are reviewed below in Chapter 2 and the appendix to Chapter 6, respectively.

3. Williams, B. (1983b). For more references on this *see* section 4.1.

4. Kaldor, N. (1932). The emphasis is mine.

5. The most prominent of the articles was that of Kaldor. Other articles include Hansen (1931, 1932) and Douglas (1930). The article by Kaldor is a review of a book on *Technological Unemployment* by E. Lederer.

6. Stoneman (1983) p. 170.

7. Freeman *et al.* (1982) pp. 188–9 and p. 75. The essence of Schumpeter's theory is contained in Chapters 3 and 4 of his *Business Cycles* (1939) and his *Theory of Economic Development* (1934). For a recent critical discussion and evaluation of neo-Schumpeterian ideas on long waves *see* Rosenberg and Frischtak (1984).

8. This interpretation is suggested by Rothwell and Zegveld (1981) pp. 221–2; it is implicit in the discussion of Freeman *et al.* 1982, as we shall see below (Chapter 4).

9. Kaldor, *ab. cit.* p. 180–1.

10. Kaldor, *ab. cit.* p. 182.

11. Hicks (1932) pp. 122 and 129–30.

12. Neary (1981) and Sinclair (1981).

13. Solow (1979 and 1980, also 1979b). For a discussion on the possibility of explaining wage–price rigidities by postulating imperfect competition *see* Stiglitz (1984).

14. Solow (1980) p. 10 and p. 8.

15. Georgescu-Roegen, N. and Fitoussi (1980) 'Structure and involuntary unemployment' in Malinvaud and Fitoussi (1980) (eds.).

PART ONE:
Product versus Process Innovation
in the Short Run: The Impact Effect on
Employment

PART ONE

Prediction versus Processing in

the Short Run: The Impact of its

Environment

SECTION A:
PROCESS INNOVATION

2 Partial Equilibrium Analysis under Perfect and Imperfect Competition

2.1 INTRODUCTION

In this chapter I explore the conditions under which a process innovation which reduces the unit cost of production for all the firms of an industry will reduce the optimal level of labour input to that industry in the short run. The phrase 'short run' indicates a period of time sufficiently short to enable one to abstract from the process of capital formation.[1] The analysis is partial equilibrium, in that I take as given a fixed inverse demand function for the industry's product.

Results based on partial equilibrium or one-sector models have recently appeared in two articles, published simultaneously in *Oxford Economic Papers* (1981). In both articles (by Neary and by Sinclair) the impact of process innovation on the short-run demand for labour is analysed. In particular, the effect on a competitive industry's demand for labour at a given real and at a given nominal wage rate is examined. In section 2.2 I review the conditions under which technical change will reduce the physical marginal product of labour, and hence labour demand at given real wages. In section 2.3 I investigate the extent to which the Neary–Sinclair analyses on the effect of technical change on labour demand at given nominal wages require modification in the context of imperfectly competitive industries. In section 2.4 I review Neary's analysis of the effect of technical change on a temporary Keynesian equilibrium in which both price and the nominal wage rate are assumed fixed.[2] Finally, section 2.5 gives a summary of the main results of this chapter, and reviews empirical work.

2.2 CONDITIONS FOR PROCESS INNOVATION TO REDUCE THE MARGINAL PRODUCT OF LABOUR

Let us consider an industry composed of n firms producing a homogeneous output $X = \Sigma_{i=1}^{n} X_i$. We write the inverse demand function for X as $p = p(X)$. Following Neary, we use the Hicksian classification of technical change, that is, technical change is classified according to the effect it has on unit input requirements at constant relative factor prices. We assume that all firms use the same constant returns technology, employing two homogeneous inputs, labour (L) and capital (K), at prices w and r respectively—with labour only variable in the short run. Assuming cost minimisation, each unit input requirement may be written as a function of w, r and a technology parameter t:

$$a_j (w,r,t) \quad j = L,K. \tag{1}$$

Unit cost c is:

$$c = c(w,r,t) = wa_L + ra_K \tag{2}$$

and since

$$a_L = \frac{L}{X} = \frac{\partial c}{\partial w} \quad \text{and} \quad a_K = \frac{K}{X} = \frac{\partial c}{\partial r} \tag{3}$$

the a_js are homogeneous of degree zero in w and r.

Now it may easily be shown (see Appendix 3) that

$$\hat{X} = \theta_L \hat{L} + \theta_K \hat{K} + q \tag{4}$$

(($\hat{\ }$) being used to denote a proportional rate of change), where

$$q = \theta_L \hat{b}_L + \theta_K \hat{b}_K \tag{5}$$

is the Hicksian measure of the *extent* of technological progress, that is, from (4), it gives the proportionate change in output when inputs are held constant, and θ_i is the share of factor i in total cost. It is also shown in Appendix 3 that:

$$\hat{c} = \theta_L \hat{w} + \theta_K \hat{r} - q \; . \tag{6}$$

To obtain (6) one must first show[3] (see Appendix 3) that

$$\hat{a}_L = -\sigma \theta_K (\hat{w} - \hat{r}) - \hat{b}_L \tag{7}$$

and

$$\hat{a}_K = \sigma \theta_L (\hat{w} - \hat{r}) - \hat{b}_K \tag{8}$$

where σ is the elasticity of substitution between labour and capital, and as is seen from (7) and (8), $\hat{b}_i$ is the proportionate reduction in a_i due to technological progress at constant factor prices. The last two equations may be combined to give the Hicksian index of the *bias* of technical change, β, which measures the proportionate change in the capital labour ratio attributable to technical change at constant factor prices:

$$\hat{K} - \hat{L} = \hat{a}_K - \hat{a}_L = \sigma (\hat{w} - \hat{r}) + \beta \tag{9}$$

where

$$\beta = \hat{b}_L - \hat{b}_K \tag{10}$$

Technical change is said to be labour saving, neutral, or capital saving, when β is positive, zero, or negative, respectively.

Now, in a competitive industry we have, from (6) (setting $\hat{c} = \hat{p}$):

$$\hat{p} - \hat{w} = -\theta_K (\hat{w} - \hat{r}) - q \tag{11a}$$

so that, using (9),

$$\hat{w} - \hat{p} = \frac{\theta_K}{\sigma} (\hat{K} - \hat{L} - \beta) + q \qquad (11b)$$

Hence, for the marginal product of labour to remain constant, when $\hat{K} = 0$, we must have

$$\hat{L} = q \frac{\sigma}{\theta_K} - \beta \qquad (12)$$

or, substituting for q and β,

$$\hat{L} = \hat{b}_L \left(\frac{\theta_L}{\theta_K} \sigma - 1 \right) + \hat{b}_K (1 + \sigma) . \qquad (12')$$

It helps in interpreting the last equation, to write down the competitive industry's short-run supply function from (4). First, using (9),

$$\hat{X} = \hat{K} - \theta_L \sigma (\hat{w} - \hat{r}) - \theta_L \beta + q$$

which on substitution from (11a) and for q and β, becomes:

$$\hat{X} = \hat{K} + \frac{\theta_L}{\theta_K} \sigma (\hat{p} - \hat{w}) + \sigma \frac{\theta_L}{\theta_K} q + \hat{b}_K . \qquad (13)$$

That is, $\sigma(\theta_L/\theta_K)$ is the short-run price elasticity of output supply. To quote Neary, equations (12) and (12') may therefore be expressed in words as follows:

In order for technological progress to reduce in the short run the level of employment corresponding to a given marginal product of labour, it is *necessary*, [from (12) and (12'), respectively] (a) that the technological progress be Hicksian labour-saving ($\beta > 0$); *and* (b) that the short-run elasticity of supply be less than unity ($\sigma(\theta_L/\theta_K) < 1$).

It should be emphasised that these conditions are necessary but not sufficient for technological progress to reduce labour demand; for example equation (12) shows that even if both conditions are met the paradoxical outcome is less likely the greater the extent of the technological progress (as measured by q). ...

It may be thought puzzling that an innovation which is defined to be labour saving (in the Hicksian sense) may or may not 'save' labour depending on the value of the elasticity of supply. There is no inconsistency however: the Hicksian definition refers to the effects of technological progress holding constant the wage–rental ratio, whereas the above result is valid only when the marginal product of labour is held constant. As the equation (11a) shows, these two conditions are not equivalent when technological progress takes place.[4]

2.3 PROCESS INNOVATION AND LABOUR DEMAND AT GIVEN NOMINAL WAGES

Part of the analysis of the papers by Neary and by Sinclair, mentioned above, is concerned with the conditions under which process innovation will increase the demand for labour at given *nominal* wages.[5] It is in particular shown in these papers that a greater than unit elasticity of demand is a necessary and sufficient condition for Hicks—neutral technical change to increase labour demand. It was, however, assumed by both these authors that product markets are perfectly competitive. The purpose of this section is to investigate the extent to which the results of these papers are changed in the context of imperfectly competitive markets.

I will re-examine the effect on an industry's optimal level of labour input in the short run, holding the nominal wage rate fixed, when technical change reduces the unit cost of production for all firms in the industry. A general formula is derived that relates changes in the optimal labour input to the bias and the extent of technical change, the elasticity of substitution between labour and capital, the shares of labour and capital in total cost, the demand elasticity and, most importantly in the present context, the price–cost margin. This last parameter summarises the role of market structure on the relation between technical change and labour demand and its value depends *inter alia* on the number of firms in the industry. This formula is then used to deduce what the effect on labour demand of technical change will be, under alternative market structures. The Neary–Sinclair condition, just mentioned, arises when the price–cost margin equals unity. It is shown that the degree of market imperfection as reflected in the price–cost margin will influence how technical change affects labour demand in a way that depends on how the elasticity of demand varies with output.

It is assumed that each firm in the industry maximises profit Π_i given by

$$\Pi_i = p(X)X_i - cX_i \quad i = 1, \ldots, n \ . \tag{14}$$

Profit maximisation requires

$$p'(X)\frac{\partial X}{\partial X_i} X_i + p(X) = c \ . \tag{15}$$

We seek a Cournot equilibrium (Nash Equilibrium in quantities)[6] where:

$$\frac{\partial X}{\partial X_i} = 1 \ . \tag{16}$$

Hence, the optimality condition for the firm i is

$$p(X) \left(1 - (X_i/\eta X)\right) = c \tag{17}$$

where $1/\eta = -p'(X)X/p$ is the inverse of the industry elasticity of demand. Then, summing over all firms in the industry we obtain the optimality condition for the industry:

$$p(X) \left[1 - \frac{1}{\eta(X)n}\right] = c(w,r,t) \ . \tag{18}$$

From (18), we may get by total differentiation:

$$Xp'(X) \left[1 - \frac{1}{\eta(X)n} - \frac{X\eta'(X)}{\eta(X)n}\right] \left(\frac{\mathrm{d}X}{X}\right) = c\left(\frac{dc}{c}\right) \tag{19}$$

so that the elasticity of output with respect to changes in the unit cost, η_c, is

$$\eta_c = -\hat{X}/\hat{c} = \eta(X)/Z(X)m \qquad (20)$$

where

$$Z(X) = 1 - 1/\eta(X)n - e(X)/n \;, \qquad (21)$$

m is the price–cost margin,

$$m = p(X)/c = (1 - (1/\eta(X)n))^{-1} \qquad (22)$$

and $e(X) = \eta'(X)X/\eta(X)$ the elasticity of elasticity.

Using (4) and (6) on (20) we obtain

$$\left(\sigma\frac{\theta_L}{\theta_K}\frac{1}{\eta_c} + 1\right)\hat{L} = -\beta + q\frac{\sigma}{\theta_K}\left(1 - \frac{1}{\eta_c}\right) \qquad (23)$$

Since $p'(X)Z(X)$ is the first derivative of the industry's marginal revenue function, for a downward-sloping demand schedule, $Z(X)$ must be positive if, as we shall assume, the marginal revenue is to have a negative slope. But if $Z(X)$ is positive, so is η_c from (20). Hence, the value inside the parenthesis on the left-hand side of (23) is positive. Hence,

$$\hat{L} \gtreqless 0 \quad \text{iff} \quad q(\sigma/\theta_K)\,[1 - (1/\eta_c)] \gtreqless \beta \qquad (24)$$

The economic intuition behind (24) is as follows. Profit maximisation (leading to condition (19)) implies that as technical change reduces unit costs output will expand; this will tend to increase labour demand. Thus, as (24) shows, for given bias, the likelihood that $\hat{L}$ will be positive is greater the greater η_c is, that is, the greater the expansion in output when unit cost is reduced. On the other hand, given the extent to which output expands as unit cost is reduced (that will depend on $\eta(X)$, $e(X)$ and n), any given output may now be produced with less labour (the more so the more labour saving the innovation) and this will tend to reduce labour demand. Thus, as (24) shows, the likelihood that $\hat{L}$ will be positive is greater the less labour saving is the innovation (that is, the smaller the value of β), for a given η_c.

The interaction of these two opposing forces in determining the demand for labour is most easily seen in the present constant returns case, where:

$$\hat{L} = \hat{X} + \hat{a}_L \tag{25}$$

$$\text{or} \quad \hat{L}/\hat{a}_L = \hat{X}/\hat{a}_L + 1 \tag{25'}$$

so that demand for labour will increase when the unit labour coefficient is reduced, if the absolute value of $\hat{X}/\hat{a}_L$ is greater than one.

Turning to a more detailed interpretation of (24), I will first deal with the effect, on the likelihood that $\hat{L}$ will be positive, of demand conditions and market structure (i.e., of $\eta(X)$, $e(X)$ and n), for given bias, and then with the conditions under which $\hat{L}$ will be positive under alternative assumptions concerning bias.

(i)   As may be seen from (24), unless the demand curve is of constant elasticity ($e(X) = 0$), market structure will affect the likelihood that $\hat{L}$ will be positive for given demand conditions. If $e(X) > 0$ (elasticity is increasing), in a cross-section of industries with the same demand elasticity, η_c, and hence the likelihood that $\hat{L}$ will be positive, will be greater the greater are $e(X)$ and m (i.e., the smaller is the number of firms in the industry). If $e(X) < 0$ (elasticity is decreasing), in a cross-section of industries with the same demand elasticity, η_c, and the likelihood that $\hat{L}$ will be positive will be smaller the greater is the absolute value of $e(X)$ and the greater is m.

On the other hand, it is important to note that, for given $e(X)$ and market structure (i.e., given n), the effect of the elasticity of demand, $\eta(X)$, on the likelihood that $\hat{L}$ will be positive is ambiguous, *unless $e(X) = 0$*; when $e(X) = 0$, $mZ(X) = 1$ and $\eta_c = \eta(X) = \eta$, so that:

$$\hat{L} \gtreqless 0 \quad \text{iff} \quad q\,\frac{\sigma}{\theta_K}\left(1 - \frac{1}{\eta}\right) \gtreqless \beta \tag{26}$$

that is, the likelihood that $\hat{L} > 0$ is greater the greater is η. When $e(X) \neq 0$, from (20), η_c will increase with $\eta(X)$ (given $e(X)$ and n) provided

$$(m - 1)\,[\eta(X)n]^2\,Z(X) > 1$$

for which it is sufficient that $\eta(X) > 1$ and $n \geq e(X)$.

To complete the present discussion we may note that in the two limiting cases of perfect competition and monopoly (24) becomes as follows:

(a)   In a *competitive industry*, $m = Z(X) = 1$ and hence $\eta_c = \eta(X)$. Thus,

$$\hat{L} \gtreqless 0 \quad \text{iff} \quad q\,\frac{\sigma}{\theta_K}\left(1 - \frac{1}{\eta(X)}\right) \gtreqless \beta \,. \qquad (27)$$

This is the Neary result. In particular, when $\beta = 0$ (technical change is Hicks neutral) an elasticity of demand greater than unity is necessary and sufficient for $\hat{L} > 0$.

(b)   When the industry is a *monopoly*, $(m - 1)/m = 1/\eta(X)$ and $mZ(X) = 1 - e(X)m$. Hence $\eta_c = \eta(X)/[1 - e(X)m]$, so that

$$\hat{L} \gtreqless 0 \quad \text{iff} \quad q\frac{\sigma}{\theta_K}\left(1 - \frac{1 - e(X)m}{\eta(X)}\right) \gtreqless \beta \qquad (28)$$

Clearly, when $\beta = 0$, a monopolist facing a constant or increasing elasticity demand curve (i.e., if $e(X) \geq 0$), will *always* increase employment—since he will always produce where $\eta(X) > 1$. (On the other hand, an oligopolist may not do so under the same circumstances, since from the profit maximisation condition it is clear that he may produce where $\eta(X) < 1$).

(ii)   Turning to the effect of the bias of innovation we first note that:

(a)   when technical change is *Hicks neutral*, that is, $\beta = 0$:

$$\hat{L} \gtreqless 0 \quad \text{iff} \quad \eta_c \gtreqless 1;$$
i.e. iff $\eta(X) \gtreqless mZ(X) = 1 - (m - 1)\eta(X)e(X)$.

(b)   when technical change is *capital saving*, that is, $\beta < 0$:

$$\hat{L} \gtreqless 0 \quad \text{iff} \quad \eta_c \gtreqless 1/(1 - \theta_K \beta/q\sigma) \ .$$

(c)   when technical change is *labour saving*, that is, $\beta > 0$, it is necessary (though not sufficient) for $\hat{L} > 0$ that:

$$\eta_c > 1 \quad and \quad \frac{\theta_K \beta}{\sigma q} \leq 1.$$

From (12), the second condition will be satisfied provided technical change does not reduce the marginal product of labour.

Thus, unless technical change is biased, σ, θ_L and q have no influence on the sign of $\hat{L}$ (that depends entirely on $\eta(X)$, $e(X)$ and n); to put it another way, when $\beta = 0$, $\eta_c > 1$ is a necessary and sufficient condition for $L > 0$. It is easy to see why this is so. From (25) and (20):

$$\hat{L}/\hat{a}_L = -\eta_c \ (\hat{c}/\hat{a}_L) + 1 \tag{29}$$

and from (5), (6) and (7), at given factor prices,

$$\hat{c} \gtreqless \hat{a}_L \quad \text{iff} \quad \beta \lesseqgtr 0 \ . \tag{30}$$

Thus, when technical change is Hicks neutral ($\beta = 0$), $\hat{c} = \hat{a}_L$, hence $\hat{X}/\hat{a}_L = \hat{X}/\hat{c} = -\eta_c$ and $\hat{L}/\hat{a}_L = 1 - \eta_c$, that is, demand for labour increases if the proportional increase in output is greater than the proportional reduction in unit costs.

When technical change is capital saving because, from (30), $\hat{c} > \hat{a}_L$, a value of η_c that is less than unity (to an extent that decreases with σ, q and θ_L) may be compatible with an increase in employment.

Finally, when technical change is labour saving, because, from (30), $\hat{c} < \hat{a}_L$, η_c must be greater than unity (to an extent that decreases with q, σ and θ_L) for there to be an increase in employment (even assuming that the marginal product of labour has not been reduced).

2.4 THE EFFECT OF PROCESS INNOVATION ON A TEMPORARY KEYNESIAN EQUILIBRIUM

I will examine, in this section, the effect of technical change on a temporary Keynesian equilibrium with w and p fixed. This effect may be analysed by using Figure 2.1 below (replicated from Neary). In the lower quadrant of Figure 2.1 I have drawn production functions and in the upper a demand for labour curve, V. Figure 2.1 is assumed to represent a temporary Keynesian equilibrium at fixed p and market wage $w = \bar{w}$. At $\bar{w}$, firms have a notional labour demand of OA, but they face a sales constraint in the goods market of $\bar{X}$, so that their effective demand for labour is only OB. The initial temporary equilibrium with rationing of firms in the goods market and households in the labour

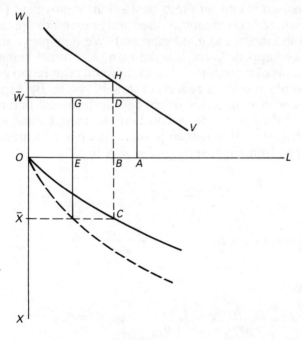

Figure 2.1

market is, here, represented by points C and D, the latter being off the firms' labour demand schedule.

Technological progress has two effects: it shifts the production function inwards, as shown by the broken line; and, as we saw in section 2.3 above, it may shift the labour demand schedule to the right or to the left. Assume for the moment that the labour demand schedule does not shift so far to the left as to intersect $\bar{w}D$ at or to the left of G. Then, this curve's shift does not affect the firms' behaviour (since their notional demand for labour remains above their effective demand that is now reduced to OE). The initial reduction in effective labour demand, from OB to OE, gives rise to a deflationary multiplier effect which eventually reduces employment below OE. Hence, in a Keynesian temporary equilibrium with both good and labour markets in excess supply, technological progress must reduce employment.

To prove this we *assumed* that V does not shift to the left so far as to cut $\bar{w}D$ at or to the left of G. Were this to happen Keynesian would turn into classical unemployment (a situation where firms are unrationed and households are rationed in both labour and good markets). We now prove that this cannot happen. Were it to happen, a notional demand for OE units of labour by firms, the amount required to produce X, would require a reduction in w below $\bar{w}$. By expressing changes in w in terms of changes in technical parameters, and holding p, K and X constant, we may deduce whether this happens. If $\hat{w}$ is then positive, it cannot happen.

Now, from (11), setting $\hat{K} = \hat{p} = 0$,

$$\hat{w} = \frac{\theta_K}{\sigma}(-\hat{L} - \beta) + q \ .$$

But from (4), if $\hat{K} = 0$, $\hat{L} = \dfrac{\hat{X} - q}{\theta_L}$

so that

$$\hat{w} = -\frac{\theta_K}{\sigma\theta_L}\hat{X} + \left(\frac{\theta_K}{\sigma\theta_L} + 1\right)q - \frac{\theta_K}{\sigma}\beta$$

and, substituting for q and β,

$$\hat{w} = -\frac{\theta_K}{\sigma\theta_L}\hat{X} + q + \frac{\theta_K}{\sigma\theta_L}\hat{b}_K .$$

Hence, if $\hat{X} = 0$

$$\hat{w} = q + \frac{\theta_K}{\sigma\theta_L}\hat{b}_K > 0 ,$$

which is what we wished to prove.

2.5 SUMMARY

In this chapter I have shown that the effect of cost-reducing process innovation on an industry's labour demand, in the short run (with labour the only variable factor), is such that:

(1) If the industry is competitive, its labour demand at given real wages may be reduced if the technical change is Hicksian labour saving and the short-run price elasticity of output supply is less than unity.

(2) A greater than unity value of the elasticity of demand is necessary and sufficient for Hicks-neutral technical change to increase a competitive industry's labour demand at given nominal wages.

(3) Only when the demand curve is of constant elasticity, market structure has no influence on whether technical change will increase or decrease the optimal value of the labour input. When it is of increasing (decreasing) elasticity, the likelihood that technical change increases labour demand is greater (smaller) the more monopolistic is the market structure, and the greater the absolute value of $e(X)$. For given market structure and $e(X)$, the likelihood that $\hat{L} > 0$ is greater the greater is the elasticity of demand, given that the latter is greater than unity and $e(X)$ is small. The effects of the elasticity of substitution, the extent of technological progress and the value of the labour share in total cost are ambiguous depending on the

bias of the technical progress. These parameters have
no influence on the sign of $\hat{L}$ when technical change is
Hicks neutral. The greater (smaller) their value the
more it is likely that $\hat{L}$ will be positive following
labour (capital) saving technological progress.
(4) In a Keynesian temporary equilibrium with both good
    and labour markets in excess supply technological
    progress must reduce employment.

Empirical Work on the impact of technological progress
on employment at the industry level is limited. One extensive study for the UK, however, is that by Wragg and
Robertson (1978), summarised by Stoneman.[7] According to
this study there is, after 1950, 'a positive relationship
between the growth of productivity and employment in
retail distribution', but not for manufacturing, 'and overall
[there is not] a statistically significant relationship between
growth rates of productivity and employment.[8] As also
noted by Stoneman, these results can be said to reflect the
theory discussed above, according to which the effect of
technical change on an industry's optimal level of labour
input depends on the elasticity of demand and of substitution between factors, the bias of the technical change, and
the structure of the industry, and cannot be signed unless
these are known.[9]

APPENDIX 1

In this Appendix I provide a brief summary of the work of
Sinclair (1980), Stoneman (1983) and Stoneman and Waterson (1984).

Sinclair's (one-sector macro-economic) analysis is rather
less general for our purposes than Neary's (reviewed above),
being based on a Constant Elasticity of Substitution (CES)
production function. Its other chief characteristics are:
(a) An examination of the implications of wage regimes
    other than the ones associated with a fixed real or
    nominal wage rate; in particular, Sinclair considers
    the implications of a fixed wage share and of the
    money wage rate being log-linear in the price level.

(b) The distinction between the effect of technical change on labour demand and its effect on employment by assuming that a worker's hours of work are related to the real wage rate per hour; this is of course inessential when one considers the effect on employment of technical change at given real wages, but makes it less likely that technical change will reduce employment at given nominal wages *if* a rise in *real* wages induces a fall in each worker's hours of work. (In the next Appendix I will make clear how the present work is related to that of Sinclair.)

Chapter 11 of Stoneman (1983) also contains an analysis of the effect of process innovation at the firm and industry level. Whilst certain of his assumptions make this analysis less general than my (or Neary's) (the use of Cobb–Douglas or CES production functions and constant elasticity demand functions, the fact that is restricted mostly to neutral change, and that it does not include a treatment of imperfectly competitive industries, other than monopoly) a part of it deals with issues not covered above.

Following the work of M. Brown, Stoneman examines the case where both factors are variable, using a CES production function, a constant elasticity demand function, $p = H_0 q^{-1/\eta}$, and constant (and equal) elasticity factor supply functions. He shows that Hicks-neutral technological progress will increase employment provided

$$\frac{1/\eta - 1}{v(1 - 1/\eta) - \epsilon} > 0 \tag{A}$$

where v represents returns to scale and $\epsilon = 1 + 1/\eta_s$, $\eta_s(>0)$ being the elasticity of supply for both factors. Thus, with constant (or decreasing) returns to scale there will be an increase in employment provided $\eta > 1$, that is, there is no change in the result obtained above in section 2.3. Further, given $\eta > 1$, and 'if we consider an increase in H_0 to represent product innovation' (Stoneman, *ab. cit.* p. 156), equation (A) guarantees that such an increase will increase employment.

Finally, Stoneman (*ab. cit.* pp. 156–9) examines the case where the new technology is diffused slowly and shows that, as there is an increase in the number of firms in a competitive industry introducing a cost-reducing innovation, 'each firm switching from old to new technology experiences an increase in output, remaining non-users suffer declines in output, but total industry output increases and price declines' (p. 158). However the author does not, in this case, obtain the employment effect. In a more recent analysis (with Waterson (1984)), Stoneman examines whether or not the level of employment in a oligopoly producing a homogeneous good changes monotonically as diffusion of a cost-reducing process innovation proceeds. The answer will in general be 'no': the level of employment may be reduced and then increased (perhaps to a higher level in the new equilibrium) as the number of firms that adopt the innovation increases. Though the assumptions of identical firms and no entry are fundamental to this analysis it certainly indicates the importance of studying diffusion paths: doing so brings out the point that technical-change-induced reductions in labour demand are much more likely than comparative static predictions would suggest.

APPENDIX 2

In this Appendix I show that the results of Chapter 2 are unaffected when the Hicksian classification of bias is not used. For example, following Sinclair, one may use a CES production function of the form

$$X = T \left[\delta_K (A_K K)^{\sigma - 1/\sigma} + \delta_L (A_L L)^{\sigma - 1/\sigma} \right]^{\sigma/\sigma - 1}$$

where $\delta_K = 1 - \delta_L$, T is a Hicks-neutral technology parameter, A_K a Solow-neutral technology parameter and A_L a Harrod-neutral technology parameter. Technological progress is registered by a rise in at least one of these parameters. It can be easily shown (from total differentiation of the profit maximisation condition w/p = marginal product of labour) that in this case equation (12′) is replaced by

$$\hat{L} = \frac{\sigma}{\theta_K}\hat{T} + \hat{A}_K + \hat{A}_L\left(\frac{\sigma}{\theta_K} - 1\right) \tag{A}$$

so that, to quote Sinclair (pp. 4–5),

(i) pure capital-augmenting technical progress—if this is defined as an increase only in the capital-efficiency index, A_k—must raise the demand for labour equiproportionately;
(ii) pure Hicks-neutral technical progress must raise the demand for labour, in the proportion of the ratio of the elasticity of substitution to the profit share;
(iii) pure labour-augmenting technical progress—if this is defined as an increase only in the Harrod neutral, or labour efficiency index, A_L—is ambiguous in its effect. It will raise or cut the demand for labour depending on whether or not the elasticity of substitution exceeds the profit share.

To show that these amount to a condition similar to Neary's (mentioned in 2.2 in the text), one must, as in the text, obtain the short-run supply function. To get this, first totally differentiate the production function to obtain $\hat{X} = \hat{T} + \theta_K(\hat{A}_K + \hat{K}) + \theta_L(\hat{A}_L + \hat{L})$.

The extent of technological progress is now:

$$q = \hat{T} + \theta_K\hat{K} + \theta_L\hat{L} , \tag{B}$$

so that,

$$\hat{X} = q + \hat{K} - \theta_L(\hat{K} - \hat{L}) . \tag{C}$$

And, totally differentiating the profit maximisation condition $r/w = MP_K/MP_L$ (MP = marginal product), we get:

$$\hat{K} - \hat{L} = (\sigma - 1)(\hat{A}_K - \hat{A}_L) + \sigma(\hat{w} - \hat{r}) . \tag{D}$$

Substituting equation (11a)— of the text—into (D) and the resulting equation into (C) gives the short-run supply function

$$\hat{X} = \hat{K} + q\left(1+\sigma\frac{\theta_L}{\theta_K}\right) - \theta_L(\sigma-1)(\hat{A}_K-\hat{A}_L) + \sigma\frac{\theta_L}{\theta_K}(\hat{p}-\hat{w})$$

indicating that $\sigma\,\theta_L/\theta_K$ is the short-run price elasticity of output supply. Since equation (A) may be rewritten as

$$\hat{L} = \hat{A}_L\left(\sigma\frac{\theta_L}{\theta_K} - 1\right) + (\hat{A}_K - \hat{A}_L) + (\sigma + 1)\hat{A}_L + \frac{\sigma}{\theta_K}\hat{T}$$

it is clear that it is necessary for technical change to reduce labour demand at given real wages, that technical change is labour biased (by which I mean that $\hat{A}_K < \hat{A}_L$) *and* that the short-run price elasticity of supply output is less than unity. Also, it is clear from the last equation that these conditions are not sufficient; in particular that a reduction in labour demand is less likely the greater the extent of technical change.

Clearly, the above equations may be used to show that all the other results of Chapter 2 are unaffected when the Hicksian classification of bias is not used. It should finally be noted at this point that whilst the analysis (in this chapter) is short run, it is not difficult to see what the impact on labour demand of changes in K will be: a relative change in the capital stock will have just the same quantitative impact on L as a relative change in the Solow-neutral technology parameter A_K.

APPENDIX 3

Proof of $\hat{a}_L = -\sigma\theta_K(\hat{w} - r) - \hat{b}_L$
(equation (7), section 2.2)

Since $a_L = L/X = \partial c/\partial w$, by total differentiation

$$\mathrm{d}a_L = \frac{\partial^2 c}{\partial w^2}\,\mathrm{d}w + \frac{\partial^2 c}{\partial w\partial r}\,\mathrm{d}r + \frac{\partial^2 c}{\partial w\partial t}\,\mathrm{d}t\ . \tag{A1}$$

Since input demand functions are homogeneous of degree zero in input prices, by Euler's theorem

$$\frac{\partial^2 c}{\partial w^2} = -\frac{r}{w}\frac{\partial^2 c}{\partial w \partial r} .$$

Further, making use of the elasticity of substitution formula

$$\sigma = \frac{c}{(\partial c/\partial w)}\frac{(\partial^2 c/\partial w \partial r)}{(\partial c/\partial w)(\partial c/\partial r)}$$

and

$$\theta_L = \frac{\partial c}{\partial w}\frac{w}{c} , \quad \theta_K = \frac{\partial c}{\partial r}\frac{r}{c}$$

and denoting by

$$-\hat{b}_L = \frac{1}{a_L}\frac{\partial}{\partial t}\left(\frac{\partial c}{\partial w}\right)dt = \frac{1}{a_L}\frac{\partial}{\partial t}(a_L)dt$$

we obtain by substitution into (A1) the desired formula. We may similarly show that $\hat{a}_K = \sigma\theta_L(\hat{w} - \hat{r}) - \hat{b}_K$.

Proof of $\hat{c} = \theta_L \hat{w} + \theta_K \hat{r} - q$
(equation (6), section 2.2)

Since $c = wa_L + ra_K$, by total differentiation

$$dc = \hat{w}(wa_L) + \hat{r}(ra_K) + \hat{a}_L(wa_L) + \hat{a}_K(ra_K) .$$

And using $\theta_L = wa_L/c$ and $\theta_K = ra_K/c$, plus the formulae obtained above for $\hat{a}_L$ and $\hat{a}_K$, we obtain by substitution:

$$\hat{c} = \hat{w}\theta_L + \hat{r}\theta_K - \theta_L\hat{b}_L - \theta_K\hat{b}_K = \hat{w}\theta_L + \hat{r}\theta_K - q .$$

Proof of $\hat{X} = \theta_L \hat{L} + \theta_K \hat{K} + q$
(equation (4), section 2.2)
Definitionally, $\hat{X} = \hat{L} - \hat{a}_L = \theta_L\hat{L} + (1 - \theta_L)\hat{L} + \theta_K\hat{K} - \theta_K\hat{K} + \theta_K\sigma(\hat{w} - \hat{r}) + \hat{b}_L$

Now, $\hat{a}_K = \hat{a}_L = \hat{K} - \hat{L} = \sigma(\hat{w} - \hat{r}) + \beta$, where $\beta = \hat{b}_L - \hat{b}_K$.

Hence, $\hat{X} = \theta_L \hat{L} + \theta_K \hat{K} + \theta_L \hat{b}_L + \theta_K \hat{b}_K = \theta_L \hat{L} + \theta_K \hat{K} + q$ by substitution.

APPENDIX 4

The Case of One Factor with Constant Returns
This case is examined for ready comparison of the current with the results of Chapter 3 where we shall assume that only one factor, labour, is used under a constant returns technology.

Assume that only labour, L, is used to produce X; a units of labour are required to produce a unit of X. Hence, $c = wa$ and $\hat{c} = \hat{a}$ and since $aX = L$, $\hat{a} = \hat{L} - \hat{X}$. Hence condition (17) now becomes:

$$[- mZ(X)/\eta(X)] \, (\hat{L} - \hat{a}) = \hat{a}$$

or

$$[mZ(X)/\eta(X)] \, (\hat{L}/\hat{a}) = -1 + (mZ(X)/\eta(X)) \ .$$

Hence,

$$\hat{L}/\hat{a} \gtreqless 0 \quad \text{iff} \quad \eta(X) \lesseqgtr mZ(X) \qquad \qquad (A2)$$

or, since $\eta_c = \eta(X)/mZ(X)$,

$$\hat{L}/\hat{a} \gtreqless 0 \quad \text{iff} \quad \eta_c \lesseqgtr 1 \ . \qquad \qquad (A2')$$

That is, a reduction in a will increase L if η_c is greater than unity, as in the Hicks-neutral case. And, of course, all the propositions in the text relating to Hicks-neutral technical change apply in this case too.

NOTES

1. This is a rather artificial assumption given the usually long periods required for diffusion processes to occur. On the other hand, work that allows the capital stock to be variable (reviewed in Appendix 1) has not produced results in variance with those discussed below.
2. I extend this analysis to the long run in Part Two of the present work, where I examine the *sequence* of temporary equilibria generated by process innovation.
3. The following half page follows closely Neary, *ab. cit.* pp. 224–5. In Appendix 1 of this chapter I provide a summary of work by Sinclair (1981) and Stoneman (1983) that is related to the issues examined here.
4. The above results are unaffected when the Hicksian classification of bias is not used. *See* Appendix 2 of this chapter for a demonstration of this.
5. At given w/p and K, as can be seen from (12'), L depends only on technical parameters, being independent of demand conditions. Again, as can be seen from (13) at a given w/p and K the short-run supply schedule is a vertical line that shifts with technological progress; hence, the increase in X is independent of demand conditions. At a given w on the other hand (and a given K) supply depends on p and the increase in X, and change in L, will depend on the elasticity of demand.
6. We could alternatively, have followed Seade (1980) and assumed that the value of the conjectural variations lies between 0 (the Cournot assumption) and unity (the firm expects its rival to respond fully to a change in its output). This would not alter the results that follow: Seade's assumption is employed in a recent analysis that also deals with the influence of technical change on an oligopolistic industry's factor demands. In this, technical change is assumed to be capital augmenting, and free entry and economies of scale are allowed (Dobbs *et al.*, 1983).
7. Stoneman (1983), Chapter 11, pp. 161–5; *see also* Freeman et al. (1982).
8. Stoneman *ab. cit.*, p. 165.
9. This conclusion is strengthened by available evidence from case studies of particular industries; *see* Table II.6, p. 229, in Rothwell and Zegveld (1981).

3 The Impact of Process Innovation in a General Equilibrium Model under Imperfect Competition

3.1 INTRODUCTION

Having examined, in Chapter 2, the partial equilibrium effect on employment of process innovation, in the present chapter I turn to an analysis of the general equilibrium effect on employment (or, the effect on the aggregate level of employment) of cost-reducing technical change in the short run, under constant returns. Homothetic preferences are assumed for most of the analysis.

An assertion often made in empirical literature is that the higher the elasticity of demand for the product of an industry, the greater is the likelihood of employment creation following the introduction of cost-reducing process innovation in that industry.[1] This assertion received theoretical backing from the analysis of the previous chapter. It is important, however, to know whether, following technical change that is specific to a particular industry and tends to increase labour demand in that industry, there will also be an increase in *aggregate* labour demand and employment (once, that is, repercussions with other sectors have been taken into account).

Now, I show below that the value of demand elasticities is crucial in determining whether the general equilibrium effect is favourable or not. However, in contrast to what is the case in a partial equilibrium setting, it is not the absolute size of demand elasticities that matters. This may seem counterintuitive. In a recent work on the subject (Heffernan, 1980) it is stated that if the effect of technical change is examined in a general equilibrium context so that 'repercussions with other sectors are introduced, awkward problems arise; for example: a high elasticity of demand for the product benefiting from technical progress implies a fall in demand and employment elsewhere. The overall employment effect may therefore be unfavourable'.[2]

What in fact we find is that when technical change is sector specific a high elasticity of demand for the product of the sector benefiting from it may not lead to a reduction in employment elsewhere. If the sector's elasticity of demand is greater than that of the other sector there will be an increase in aggregate labour demand whatever the absolute size of demand elasticities. When technical change is general neither the absolute nor the relative size of demand elasticities matters.

Before we conclude the present introductory section some general remarks are in order concerning the following analysis. The use of a general equilibrium model enables one to incorporate into the analysis and examine the implications of a very important aspect of reality: the sector specificity of technical change. Indeed it is for the analysis of sector-specific technical change that general equilibrium is especially needed. Most of the analysis that follows concentrates on sector-specific technical change.

In the next three sections of this chapter I describe how technical change affects labour demand at given aggregate nominal income and nominal wage rate. I term this the impact effect of technological progress on labour demand. In section 5 I introduce labour supply considerations and look at the effect of technical change on labour market equilibrium, and the full employment ceiling.

In the next section, after describing the general assumptions used throughout this chapter, I will look at the effect of general technical change (i.e., of a change that reduces unit cost equiproportionally for all sectors). As we shall see, the effect of such change may be described in quite general terms. The effect of sector-specific technical change, on the other hand, is much more complicated. It is examined in sections 3 and 4. Section 4 contains the main results of this chapter. Once we relate changes in the unit labour coefficient to changes in the optimal level of labour input, and look at the special case of symmetric equilibria (in section 3), we proceed to examine, in considerable detail, the general effect of sector-specific technical change in section 4, using demand functions arising from CES utility functions. (Two more cases—that of constant elasticity demand functions, and those derived from the 'circular road' model of product differentiation, following Weitzman—are examined in Appendix 2).

3.2 A MODEL: THE EFFECT OF GENERAL TECHNICAL CHANGE

The general equilibrium model that will be employed below may be characterised by the following set of general assumptions:

A1. The equilibrium concept used will be a Nash equilibrium in prices, for an economy in which two firms produce two substitute consumer goods.

A2. Only one factor, labour, is employed under a constant returns technology; a_i will denote the unit labour coefficient in sector (firm) i, $i = 1,2$.

A3. The level of nominal aggregate expenditure is fixed exogenously at Y.

Thus we will be concerned with the *impact effect* of a technical change, holding aggregate nominal expenditure constant. Thus, the policy implications of the appearance of unemployment as a consequence of technical change, in this sort of setting, is that such changes need to be accompanied by an offsetting expansionary policy.

I will further show that (through the expansion in labour supply as a result of the technical change induced reduction in prices) the *full employment ceiling* which can be attained by means of such policies is unambiguously raised by technical change. Thus our main focus lies in the divergence between the potential rise in the level of employment, and the short-run impact on employment, as a result of technical change.

Finally, I will be assuming for most of the analysis that follows that:

A4. Preferences are homothetic.

Now let X_i, p_i and L_i denote output, price and employment in sector i, respectively, and L the aggregate employment level, (and labour demand, unless otherwise stated). In long-run zero profit equilibrium, with the number of firms endogenously determined, employment is fixed at Y/w, w being the nominal wage rate (Y being, then, the wage bill), that is, employment is independent of changes in a_i. In the short run, with the number of firms fixed (as already mentioned, we assume one firm in each sector), whether or not total labour demand is affected by technical change that is general can be analysed in the following way.

Since it is always true that $p_1X_1 + p_2X_2 = Y$ and that

$$L_i = a_iX_i, \quad i = 1,2; \quad L = L_1 + L_2 \tag{1}$$

it follows that

$$L = \frac{a_2}{p_2}Y - L_1\left(\frac{a_2p_1}{a_1p_2} - 1\right). \tag{2}$$

In a symmetric equilibrium, $a_1 = a_2 = a$ and $p_1 = p_2 = p$, so that then

$$L = \frac{aY}{p}. \tag{3}$$

The effect of general technical change on a symmetric equilibrium will be to reduce a to a' and thus p to p' and L to $L' = a'Y/p'$, that is, $L = L'$ iff $(a'/p') = (a/p)$. Since p/a is expenditure required to employ a man (unit of labour), with Y fixed, technical change will not affect (increase, decrease) labour demand if it does not affect (decrease, increase) the amount of expenditure required to employ a man. From the optimality condition $p[1 - (1/\eta)] = wa$ where η is the elasticity of demand, p/a will be unaffected between symmetric equilibria if η is unaffected. η will in turn be unaffected if it is constant (demand functions are of constant elasticity), or if the elasticity depends on relative prices only (in symmetric equilibria the ratio of sector prices being unity), as would be the case if preferences were homothetic. If η decreases (increases) with absolute prices, p/a will increase (decrease) between symmetric equilibria, labour demand at given nominal wages being thereby reduced (increased). Note that the *value* of η does not affect the outcome: with Y fixed, everything depends on what happens to p/a between the old and new equilibrium; this in turn depends on how η *changes* between the new and old equilibrium. This remains true if the original equilibrium is not symmetric, a case to which I now turn.

From (1), (2) and the optimality conditions:

$$p_1\left(1 - \frac{1}{\eta_{11}}\right) = wa_1; \quad p_2\left(1 - \frac{1}{\eta_{22}}\right) = wa_2 \qquad (4)$$

where

$$\eta_{11} = - \frac{\partial X_1 p_1}{\partial p_1 X_1} \quad \text{and} \quad \eta_{22} = - \frac{\partial X_2}{\partial p_2} \frac{p_2}{X_2} \qquad (5)$$

it may be shown that under homothetic preferences *general technical change will not affect the total labour demand or its distribution between sectors.*

To show this we first note that homothetic preferences imply that we may write the demand functions for X_1 and X_2 as

$$X_1 = X_1(p_1, p_2, Y) \qquad (6)$$

and $X_2 = X_2(p_1, p_2, Y),$ $\qquad (7)$

that is, as independent of income distribution. Further they imply that income elasticity is unity so that

$$\eta_{11} - \eta_{12} = 1 = \eta_{22} - \eta_{21} \qquad (8)$$

where

$$\eta_{12} = \frac{\partial X_1}{\partial p_2} \frac{p_2}{X_1} \quad \text{and} \quad \eta_{21} = \frac{\partial X_2}{\partial p_1} \frac{p_1}{X_2} \qquad (9)$$

are the cross elasticities. Totally differentiating (6) and (7) holding Y constant gives:[3]

$$\hat{X}_1 = -\eta_{11}\hat{p}_1 + \eta_{12}\hat{p}_2 \tag{10}$$

and

$$\hat{X}_2 = -\eta_{22}\hat{p}_2 + \eta_{21}\hat{p}_1 . \tag{11}$$

Since

$$\hat{L}_1 = \hat{a}_1 + \hat{X}_1 \tag{12}$$

$$\hat{L}_2 = \hat{a}_2 + \hat{X}_2 \tag{13}$$

It follows that

$$\hat{L}_1 = \hat{a}_1 - \eta_{11}\hat{p}_1 + \eta_{12}\hat{p}_2 \tag{14}$$

and

$$\hat{L}_2 = \hat{a}_2 - \eta_{22}\hat{p}_2 + \eta_{21}\hat{p}_1 . \tag{15}$$

On the other hand, totally differentiating the optimality conditions (4), holding w constant, gives

$$\hat{p}_1(\eta_{11} - 1 + e_{11}) + e_{12}\hat{p}_2 = (\eta_{11} - 1)\hat{a}_1 \tag{16}$$

and

$$\hat{p}_2(\eta_{22} - 1 + e_{22}) + e_{21}\hat{p}_1 = (\eta_{22} - 1)\hat{a}_2 \tag{17}$$

which solve to give

$$\hat{p}_1 = \frac{(\eta_{11} - 1)\hat{a}_1(\eta_{22} - 1 + e_{22}) - e_{12}(\eta_{22} - 1)\hat{a}_2}{(\eta_{11} - 1 + e_{11})(\eta_{22} - 1 + e_{22}) - e_{12}e_{21}} \tag{18}$$

and

$$\hat{p}_2 = \frac{(\eta_{22} - 1)\hat{a}_2(\eta_{11} - 1 + e_{11}) - e_{21}(\eta_{11} - 1)\hat{a}_1}{(\eta_{22} - 1 + e_{22})(\eta_{11} - 1 + e_{11}) - e_{21}e_{12}} \tag{19}$$

where

$$e_{ij} = \frac{\partial \eta_{ij}}{\partial p_j} \frac{p_j}{\eta_{ij}} \quad i \neq j; \quad i, j = 1,2 . \tag{20}$$

To say that an elasticity depends only on relative prices means that the effect on an elasticity of a given proportionate change in p_i must be equal to and opposite to that of the same change in p_j, that is,

$$e_{11} = -e_{12} \quad \text{and} \quad e_{22} = -e_{21} \qquad (21)$$

Thus under homothetic preferences (18) and (19) become

$$\hat{p}_1 = \frac{(\eta_{11} - 1)\hat{a}_1(\eta_{22} - 1 + e_{22}) + e_{11}(\eta_{22} - 1)\hat{a}_2}{(\eta_{11} - 1)(\eta_{22} - 1 + e_{22}) + e_{11}(\eta_{22} - 1)} \qquad (18')$$

$$\hat{p}_2 = \frac{(\eta_{22} - 1)\hat{a}_2(\eta_{11} - 1 + e_{11}) + e_{22}(\eta_{11} - 1)\hat{a}_1}{(\eta_{22} - 1)(\eta_{11} - 1 + e_{11}) + e_{22}(\eta_{11} - 1)} \qquad (19')$$

That is, under homothetic preferences general technical change implies that:

(i) $\hat{p}_1 = \hat{p}_2$
(ii) $(\hat{p}_1/\hat{a}_1) = (\hat{p}_2/\hat{a}_2) = 1$, that is, (p_1/a_1), (p_2/a_2) remain unchanged

Using (i) and (ii) on (14), (15) and taking account of (8):

(iii) $\hat{L}_1 = \hat{L}_2 = 0$, that is, the distribution of labour demand is unchanged, so that from (10), (11) we get:
(iv) $\hat{X}_1 = -\hat{a}_1$ and $\hat{X}_2 = -\hat{a}_2$

Finally, (ii) and (iii) show, using (2), that:

(v) General technical change will leave total labour demand unchanged.

3.3 SECTOR-SPECIFIC TECHNICAL CHANGE: EFFECT ON SYMMETRIC EQUILIBRIA

Let us now assume that technical change is sector specific, occurring in sector 1 only, that is, $\hat{a}_2 = 0$. From (18') and (19'), in this case:

$$\hat{p}_1 = \frac{(\eta_{11} - 1)\hat{a}_1(\eta_{22} - 1 + e_{22})}{(\eta_{11} - 1)(\eta_{22} - 1 + e_{22}) + e_{11}(\eta_{22} - 1)} \qquad (18'')$$

and

$$\hat{p}_2 = \frac{e_{22}(\eta_{11} - 1)\hat{a}_1}{(\eta_{22} - 1)(\eta_{11} - 1 + e_{11}) + e_{22}(\eta_{11} - 1)}$$

$$= \frac{e_{22}\hat{p}_1}{\eta_{22} - 1 + e_{22}} \tag{19''}$$

So it follows that, with sector-specific change in sector 1, if $e_{11}, e_{22} > 0$ (as is the case with CES utility functions),

(i) $\hat{p}_2 < \hat{p}_1$

and

(ii) $(\hat{p}_1/\hat{a}_1) < 1$, that is, (p_1/a_1) is increased, whilst since $\hat{a}_2 = 0$, (p_2/a_2) is decreased.

Now, from (14), substituting the second equation of (19'') we obtain

$$\frac{\hat{L}_1}{\hat{a}_1} = 1 - \frac{\hat{p}_1}{\hat{a}_1} \left[\frac{\eta_{11}(\eta_{22} - 1 + e_{22}) + \eta_{12}e_{21}}{\eta_{22} - 1 + e_{22}} \right] \tag{22}$$

which, using (18'') gives:

$$\frac{\hat{L}_1}{\hat{a}_1} = 1 - \left[\frac{\eta_{11}(\eta_{11} - 1)(\eta_{22} - 1 + e_{22}) + \eta_{12}e_{21}(\eta_{11} - 1)}{(\eta_{22} - 1 + e_{22})(\eta_{11} - 1) + e_{11}(\eta_{22} - 1)} \right] . \tag{22'}$$

And, from (15), substituting (19'') and then (18''),

$$\frac{\hat{L}_2}{\hat{a}_1} = \frac{(\eta_{11} - 1)[\eta_{21}(\eta_{22} - 1 + e_{22}) + \eta_{22}e_{21}]}{(\eta_{22} - 1 + e_{22})(\eta_{11} - 1) + e_{11}(\eta_{22} - 1)} . \tag{23}$$

Finally,

$$\hat{L} = \frac{L_1}{L}\hat{L}_1 + \frac{L_2}{L}\hat{L}_2 = s_{L1}\hat{L}_1 + s_{L2}\hat{L}_2 \tag{24}$$

where

$$s_{Li} = \frac{L_i}{L}$$

so that,

$$\frac{\hat{L}}{\hat{a}_1} = s_{L1}\left(\frac{\hat{L}_1 + \hat{L}_2}{\hat{a}_1}\right) + (s_{L2} - s_{L1})\frac{\hat{L}_2}{\hat{a}_1} \, . \qquad (24')$$

The Effect on Symmetric Equilibria
In a symmetric equilibrium $a_1 = a_2$, $p_1 = p_2$, $\eta_{11} = \eta_{22}$, $\eta_{12} = \eta_{21}$, $e_{22} = e_{11}$. It is then easily shown that

$$\frac{\hat{L}_1}{\hat{a}_1} = -\frac{\hat{L}_2}{\hat{a}_1} \quad \text{that is,} \quad \frac{\hat{L}_2 + \hat{L}_1}{\hat{a}_1} = 0 \, .$$

Since in symmetric equilibrium $s_{L1} = s_{L2}$, we have from (24') that, under homothetic preferences, the effect on symmetric equilibrium of

    (iii) Sector-specific technical change leaves total labour demand unchanged (as does general technical change).

3.4   SECTOR-SPECIFIC TECHNICAL CHANGE: EFFECT ON NON-SYMMETRIC EQUILIBRIA

In this section I specialise to the case of a CES utility function. I assume that there are N' consumers of which N are workers and the rest are rentiers (the latter receiving all profit). Utility of consumer K from consumption is described by

$$V = (C_1^{-\alpha} + C_2^{-\alpha})^{-1/\alpha}$$

or

$$V = (C_1^{\sigma-1/\sigma} + C_2^{\sigma-1/\sigma})^{\sigma/\sigma-1} \qquad (25)$$

where $\sigma = 1/1 + \alpha$. First-order conditions for the maximisation of (25) subject to $y = p_1 C_1 + p_2 C_2$, require that

$$\frac{\partial V}{\partial C_i} = \left(\frac{V}{C_i}\right)^{1/\sigma} = \lambda p_i \; ; \quad i = 1,2 \tag{26}$$

where λ is the shadow price on the budget constraint. From equations (26) we may obtain

$$C_i = \frac{y}{p_i^\sigma A} \; ; \quad i = 1,2 \tag{27}$$

where

$$A = \frac{1}{p_1^{\sigma-1}} + \frac{1}{p_2^{\sigma-1}} \; . \tag{28}$$

Homotheticity ensures that the composition of the consumption bundle is independent of y. So let C_i^w, C_i^r, represent the consumption of good i of a worker and rentier respectively. If L workers are in employment, aggregate demand for good i would be

$$X_i = LC_i^w + (N' - N)C_i^r$$

$$\tag{29}$$

$$= \frac{Y}{p_i^\sigma A} \; ; \quad i = 1,2$$

where

$$Y = wL + (N' - N)y \; . \tag{30}$$

From (29) we get the own price and cross-price elasticities:

$$\eta_{11} = \sigma - (\sigma - 1)s_1; \quad \eta_{22} = \sigma - (\sigma - 1)s_2 \tag{31}$$

and

$$\eta_{12} = (\sigma - 1)s_2 \; ; \quad \eta_{21} = (\sigma - 1)s_1 \tag{32}$$

where

$$s_i = \frac{p_i X_i}{Y} = \frac{1}{1 + \left(\dfrac{p_i}{p_j}\right)^{\sigma-1}} \quad i,j = 1,2; \quad i \neq j \tag{32'}$$

are the shares in national income.

Also,

$$e_{11} = -e_{12} = \frac{\eta_{12}\eta_{21}}{\eta_{11}} \quad \text{and} \quad e_{22} = -e_{21} = \frac{\eta_{21}\eta_{12}}{\eta_{22}}. \tag{33}$$

Finally, since $L_i = \dfrac{a_i s_i Y}{p_i}$, it follows that

$$s_{L1} = \frac{L_1}{L} = \frac{1}{1 + \dfrac{a_2 s_2 p_1}{a_1 s_1 p_2}}. \tag{34}$$

From the optimality conditions (4), it follows that it must be true that (given (8)),

$$\frac{p_1 a_2}{p_2 a_1} = \frac{\eta_{21}\eta_{11}}{\eta_{12}\eta_{22}}. \tag{35}$$

Also, from equations (32):

$$\frac{s_2}{s_1} = \frac{\eta_{12}}{\eta_{21}}. \tag{36}$$

Substituting (35) and (36) into (34), we obtain

$$s_{L1} = \frac{\eta_{22}}{\eta_{11} + \eta_{22}} \quad \text{and} \quad s_{L2} = \frac{\eta_{11}}{\eta_{11} + \eta_{22}}. \tag{37}$$

Now, using equations (33) one can show that in the present case equations (22') and (23) become:

$$\frac{\hat{L}_1}{\hat{a}_1} = \frac{\eta_{22}(\eta_{21} - \eta_{11}\eta_{12})}{\eta_{22}\eta_{11} + \eta_{12}\eta_{11} + \eta_{21}\eta_{22}} \gtreqless 0 \text{ iff } \eta_{21} \gtreqless \eta_{11}\eta_{12} \tag{38}$$

and

$$\frac{\hat{L}_2}{\hat{a}_1} = \frac{\eta_{11}(\eta_{22}\eta_{21} - \eta_{11})}{\eta_{22}\eta_{11} + \eta_{12}\eta_{11} + \eta_{21}\eta_{22}} \gtreqless 0 \text{ iff } \eta_{22}\eta_{21} \gtreqless \eta_{12} \ .$$

(39)

Also,

$$\frac{\hat{L}_1 + \hat{L}_2}{\hat{a}_1} = \frac{(\eta_{22} - \eta_{11})(\eta_{11}\eta_{22} + \eta_{12} + \eta_{22})}{\eta_{22}\eta_{11} + \eta_{12}\eta_{11} + \eta_{21}\eta_{22}}$$

$$\gtreqless 0 \text{ iff } \eta_{22} \gtreqless \eta_{11}$$

(40)

and, using equations (37)–(39) into equation (24),

$$\frac{\hat{L}}{\hat{a}_1} = \frac{(\eta_{22} - \eta_{11})[\eta_{22}^2 + \eta_{11}\eta_{22} + \eta_{12}(\eta_{22} + \eta_{11})]}{(\eta_{11} + \eta_{22})(\eta_{22}\eta_{11} + \eta_{12}\eta_{11} + \eta_{21}\eta_{22})}$$

$$\gtreqless 0 \text{ iff } \eta_{22} \gtreqless \eta_{11} \ .$$

(41)

From (38)–(39) it follows that, under homothetic preferences,

(i) $\eta_{22} \lesseqgtr \eta_{11}$ is sufficient for an increase in labour demand in sector 1, and $\eta_{22} \gtreqless \eta_{11}$ is sufficient for a decrease in labour demand in sector 2.

From (41), under homothetic preferences,

(ii) sector-specific technical change occurring in sector 1 will increase (decrease) aggregate labour demand if the elasticity of demand for good 1 is greater (less) than the elasticity of demand for good 2.

That is, in deducing the general equilibrium effect on labour demand of cost-reducing technical change, the absolute value of the elasticities is not important (as is, of course, the case with the partial equilibrium effect) but their relative value is.

To interpret and clarify further these results we must remember that a sector's value of the expenditure required to employ a labour unit, p_i/a_i for sector i, is less than that of the other sector if its elasticity is greater. That is, in equilibrium, a relatively high elasticity indicates (or, is associated with) a relatively low p_i/a_i. Thus, if $\eta_{11} > \eta_{22}(\eta_{22} > \eta_{11})$, technical change occurs in, and hence shifts expenditure to, the sector where expenditure required to employ a unit of labour is low (high). This results in an increase (a decrease) in aggregate labour demand even though, in the new equilibrium, p_1/a_1 (p_2/a_2) is increased (decreased).

It may help to clarify our results further if we note that the proportional change in labour demand in sector i equals the proportional change in the share (in national income) of this sector minus the proportional change in the expenditure required to employ a labour unit in this sector, as a result of the technical change, that is, $\hat{L}_i = \hat{s}_i - (p_i/a_i)$ (obtained by totally differentiating $L_i = s_i Y/(p_i/a_i)$). Now, technical change in sector 1 increases s_1 and p_1/a_1 and decreases s_2 and p_2/a_2. So, employment in sector 1(2) will increase (decrease) if s_1 (s_2) increases (decreases) proportionally more than p_1/a_1 (p_2/a_2). Hence, implicitly will increase (decrease) if proposition (i) says that:

for the sector with the greater elasticity the proportional change in its share, as a result of technical change, is greater than the proportional change, as a result of this technical change, in the amount of expenditure required to employ a labour unit in the sector (hence, if $\eta_{11} > \eta_{22} \Rightarrow \hat{L}_1/\hat{a}_1 < 0$ whilst if $\eta_{22} > \eta_{11} \Rightarrow \hat{L}_2/\hat{a}_1 > 0$, if technical change occurs in sector 1).

It is also easily seen, from equations (38) and (39), that, it is always true that:

the absolute value of the change in labour demand in sector i (as given by the last equation above) is greater than that of sector j iff i has a higher elasticity.

This explains (40). Finally, to obtain (41), from (24) and the above, it must be true that:

the absolute value of the change in labour demand in sector i weighted by its employment share is greater than that of sector j, similarly weighted, iff i has a higher elasticity.

A final corollary of the above analysis seems worthwhile stating at this point:

by reducing the relative price and increasing the relative share of the sector affected by it, technical change that *persistently* affects the same sector will *eventually* have a negative impact on aggregate labour demand, even if initially its impact leads to an increase in this demand.

3.5   LABOUR SUPPLY: THE EFFECT OF TECHNICAL CHANGE ON LABOUR MARKET EQUILIBRIUM

Till now I have been concerned with the effect of technical change on labour demand, that is, on the optimal level of labour input at given nominal wages. To complete the analysis I will introduce, in this section, labour supply considerations and look at the effect of technical change on the labour market equilibrium.

I will now assume that each of the N workers, say worker k, decides whether to work or not depending on whether

$$U_k = V - \omega_k \tag{42}$$

is positive or negative, respectively, V being given by equation (25). The parameter ω measures the disutility from work. ω_k is, in effect, the reservation wage of worker k. It is assumed that ω is uniformly distributed over the range $0 \leq \omega \leq \bar{\omega}$ as shown in Figure 3.1; that is, the density function of $\bar{\omega}$ is

$$g(\omega) = \begin{cases} K & 0 \leq \omega \leq \bar{w} \\ \\ 0 & \text{otherwise} \end{cases}$$

so that $K\bar{\omega} = N$.

Now note that from the two optimality conditions (equations (4)), with elasticities given by equations (31) and

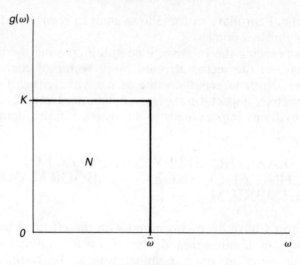

Figure 3.1

account being taken of (32') we may obtain p_1 and p_2 for given w. Given Y, X_1 and X_2 may then be obtained from equations (29), and hence labour demand ($= a_1X_1 + a_2X_2$). (Profit may then be obtained from (30).) Further, from equations (27), that is, the workers' demand functions, demands for goods 1 and 2 by a representative worker may be obtained, and hence his utility score V (from (25)). From (42) we may then obtain labour supply, which will increase with w and an equiproportionate reduction in p_1 and p_2 (holding w constant). The labour market equilibrium condition, $a_1X_1 + a_2X_2 = $ labour supply, may then be solved to give the value of w that will clear the labour market.

What was shown in the previous three sections was that under homothetic preferences the effect of general technical change is to reduce equiproportionately both p_1 and p_2, whilst sector-specific change will in general reduce p_1 more than p_2. In either case the workers' utility score, V, from consumption, is increased. The amount of labour supplied at given w is thus always increased.

The effect on the labour market equilibrium depends on what happens to the labour demand schedule. First we note that, since in our case the marginal revenue schedules are decreasing in outputs (so that an increase in w, and hence marginal cost, will decrease X_1 and X_2), demand for labour is decreasing in w.[4] Below demand and supply for labour are represented by L^d and L^s respectively. In Figure 3.2 the effect of general technical change on the labour market is depicted: as shown above, in this case $\hat{L}^d = 0$. In Figure 3.3 I depict the effect on labour market equilibrium of sector-specific change (affecting sector 1) when $\eta_{22} > \eta_{11}$, that is, when aggregate labour demand is reduced ($L^{d'}$, $L^{s'}$ are the demand and supply schedules after the technical change). An interchange in the positions of L^d and $L^{d'}$, in Figure 3.3. gives the effect of sector-specific technical change when $\eta_{22} < \eta_{11}$.

As noted at the beginning of this chapter, and as must now be clear from the above discussion, leading to Figures 3.2 and 3.3, technical change, by increasing labour supply, will raise the full employment ceiling that can be attained by means of expansionary policies. Thus, even when, as in Figure 3.3, the impact effect of sector-specific technical change is to shift the labour market equilibrium from A to B, that is, to *reduce* actual employment, were the government, say, to *maintain* total labour demand by stimulating expenditure, the equilibrium level of employment would *increase* to point C.

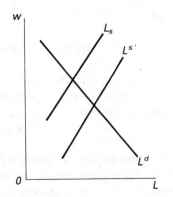
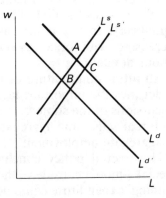

Figure 3.2: *General technical change*

Figure 3.3: *Sector-specific technical change*

3.6 CONCLUDING REMARKS

By reducing prices and thus increasing the workers' utility from consumption relative to disutility from work, technical change will increase labour supply and so raise the 'full employment ceiling'. However, its impact effect on total demand and employment is ambiguous: when technical change is general (or, balanced) so that relative prices are unaffected by it, and preferences are homothetic (so that elasticities are affected only by changes in relative prices), total labour demand is unaffected. When technical change is sector specific, it may or may not increase total demand for labour, depending on which sector is affected by the change. Generally speaking, technical change increases aggregate labour demand if it leads to a shift in expenditure to the sector where expenditure required to employ a labour unit, p/a, is least. With homothetic preferences this will occur if the sector affected by the change is the small share-high elasticity sector (this being, then, the sector with the least p/a). Technical change affecting the large share-low elasticity sector will lead to a reduction in aggregate labour demand.[5]

In Appendix 2 to this chapter I also look at the case of constant elasticities demand functions (giving the same results as above), and the case of demand functions for which elasticities *are* affected by changes in the level of absolute prices (dealing, for simplicity, only with symmetric equilibria). In the latter case we see that, with elasticity increasing with price, *general* technical change *increases* labour demand.

An interesting feature of the foregoing analysis is that it underlines the important fact, overlooked in many popular discussions of the subject, that process innovation may raise both real wages and aggregate output, while leading to a fall in aggregate employment.

The overall policy conclusion appropriate in the—very special—model considered here is that expansionary 'pump-priming' expenditure could be used to shift the economy to a 'full employment' position (a theme echoing Weitzman (1982)).[6]

Nonetheless, one should not press the implications of the foregoing analysis very far. Its limitations are self-evident. We have been concerned with the somewhat artificial exercise of examining the impact effect of technical change, holding aggregate expenditure fixed. (One might have in mind the idea of holding the money supply fixed; as I note in Appendix 1 to the present chapter, this idea underlies existing work on the subject).

The main virtue of this exercise is that it affords a very useful point of departure for two themes, to which I now turn:

(i) The first of these concerns the contrast with *product innovation*. I show that here, even the *impact effect* on employment, in the sense in which I have defined it, is favourable.

(ii) My second concern is to explore further the analysis of process innovation, but within a long-run setting. This will be the subject of Part Two below.

APPENDIX 1

This appendix provides a brief discussion of the work by Heffernan (1980). This is an M. Phil. thesis on the general equilibrium effect of process innovation. The author examines the effect of exogenous disembodied technical change on a two-consumer good, two-factor (labour and capital) closed economy, in the short run, with the capital stock, nominal wage and money stock assumed fixed, and with markets assumed to be perfectly competitive. He includes a demand for money equation (as in Sinclair (1980)) to examine the 'role of monetary macro-responses':

Technical progress in one or both sectors raises real national income and reduces the price level. The latter reduces the demand for money but the former raises it. Therefore, the *price effect* on the demand for money lowers the interest rate while the *volume effect* causes it to increase. ... [If] the volume effect outweighs the price effect.... the interest rate rises, discouraging investment expenditure. This, in turn, negatively affects the level of aggregate demand and must therefore add to the level of unemployment, if any, caused by technical change.... [In the opposite case] the lower rate of interest stimulates investment and through the rise in the level of aggregate demand will favour the aggregate level of employment (p. 74).

More relevant, from our point of view, is Heffernan's analysis using what he calls Models I and II, distinguished by the fact that in the latter a CES (rather than a Cobb–Douglas) production function is utilised with two general demand functions for the two consumer goods (of the form $Q_i = f(P_1, P_1, Q_1, Q_2 r, M)i = 1,2$, r being the rate of interest and M the money stock). This takes up Chapters 2, 3 and 4 (or two-thirds) of the thesis, the rest being introductory material plus a concluding chapter.

A general point concerning the analysis is that the great increase in complexity—as compared with the analysis of Chapter 3 above—does not seem to lead to a *compensating* increase in general results and, further, makes interpretation extremely difficult (a point reflected in the author's erroneous remarks concerning the role of demand elasticities in a general equilibrium framework, mentioned in 3.1 above). Thus, Model I, taking up most of the three central chapters, relies in order to obtain its conclusions (see table in p. 42) on *ad hoc* specification of demand and supply elasticities (pp. 29–32) to establish that the factor that is most important as a determining influence on whether technical change reduces labour demand is the value of the relative share of the sector in which the change occurs (the greater the share the greater is the likelihood of an adverse employment effect—p. 41), and fails to interpret this or relate it to the sectors' demand elasticities. Chapter 3 above may be seen as providing a simple rigorous analysis of the interrelationship between a sector's national income share, its demand elasticity and the value of the expenditure required to employ a labour unit in the sector, in determining the influence of general and sector-specific technical change on aggregate labour demand and employment.

Of less importance to relative shares (Heffernan's Model I indicates) is factor intensities: the likelihood that sector-specific technical change has an adverse effect on employment varies positively with the capital intensity of the sector where the technical change occurs and also positively (negatively) with the capital intensity of the other sector when the two goods are complements (substitutes) in demand (p. 82).

With Model II (with the elasticity of substitution between labour and capital, σ_i, for sector $i = 1,2$ not restricted to unity but with demand elasticities still parametrically specified) Heffernan also establishes the importance of σ_i itself and factor shares as determinants of the change in sectoral and aggregate levels of employment. Most importantly, 'the probability of an adverse employment effect rises with σ_i if the technical progress is Solow neutral and decreases as σ_i rises if the technical progress is of the labour augmenting variety' (p. 81). Note that, for this result, one does not require general equilibrium analysis: a similar result was established in section 2.3 above using a simpler partial equilibrium analysis (see, in particular, conclusion 3 of section 2.5).

APPENDIX 2

In this appendix two more cases are examined: the case where demand functions are of the constant elasticities type and the case of Weitzman-type demand functions. For simplicity I examine only the effect on labour demand when the initial equilibrium is symmetric.

A. Constant Elasticity Demand Functions
Demand functions are now given by

$$X_i = \frac{Y}{2(p_i^{\eta_{ii}} p_j^{-\eta_{ij}})} \; ; \quad i,j = 1, 2; \quad i \neq j$$

where $\eta_{ii} - \eta_{ij} = 1$. Since elasticities are constant $e_{11} = e_{22} = e_{12} = e_{21} = 0$. From (18) and (19) it follows that, in this case

$$\hat{p}_1 = \hat{a}_1 \quad \text{and} \quad \hat{p}_2 = \hat{a}_2$$

So, *if technical change is general*, that, is $\hat{a}_1 = \hat{a}_2 \Rightarrow \hat{p}_1 = \hat{p}_2$, and from (14) and (15) $\hat{L}_1 = \hat{L}_2 = 0$, that is, there is no change in total or in the distribution of labour demand.

If, on the other hand, *technical change is sector specific*, that is, $\hat{a}_2 = 0$, from (18), (19) it follows that $\hat{p}_1 = \hat{a}_1$ and $\hat{p}_2 = \hat{a}_2 = 0 \Rightarrow p_1/a_1, p_2/a_2$ are unaffected. From (14), (15),

$$\frac{\hat{L}_1}{\hat{a}_1} = 1 - \eta_{11} < 0 \text{ and } \frac{\hat{L}_2}{\hat{a}_1} = \eta_{21} = \eta_{22} - 1 > 0 .$$

Hence,

$$\frac{\hat{L}_1}{\hat{a}_1} + \frac{\hat{L}_2}{\hat{a}_1} = 1 - \eta_{11} + \eta_{21} = \eta_{22} - \eta_{11} .$$

B.   Weitzman-type Demand Functions

Assume now that demand functions are given by:

$$X_i = \frac{W}{2p_i} + \frac{bwW}{p_i}\left(\frac{1}{p_i} - \frac{1}{p_j}\right) + \frac{P}{2p_i}; \; i,j = 1,2 \; i \neq j^7$$

where W is the wage bill and P the profits. We have,

$$\eta_{11} = 1 + \frac{bwW}{p_1(p_1X_1)}; \quad \eta_{22} = 1 + \frac{bwW}{p_2(p_2X_2)}$$

$$\eta_{12} = \frac{bwW}{p_2(p_1X_1)}; \quad \eta_{21} = \frac{bwW}{p_1(p_2X_2)}$$

$$e_{11} = \frac{(\eta_{11} - 2)(\eta_{11} - 1)}{\eta_{11}}; \quad e_{22} = \frac{(\eta_{22} - 2)(\eta_{22} - 1)}{\eta_{22}}$$

$$e_{12} = \frac{-(\eta_{11} - 1)^2}{\eta_{11}}\frac{p_1}{p_2}; \quad e_{21} = \frac{-(\eta_{22} - 1)^2}{\eta_{22}}\frac{p_2}{p_1}.$$

In symmetric equilibrium, $p_1 = p_2$, $X_1 = X_2$ and hence,

$$\eta_{11} = \eta_{22}, \quad \eta_{12} = \eta_{21}, \quad e_{11} = e_{22}, \quad e_{12} = e_{21}$$
$$\text{and} \quad \eta_{11} - \eta_{12} = 1 = \eta_{22} - \eta_{21} .$$

General Technical Change: $\hat{a}_1 = \hat{a}_2 = \hat{a}$. From (18), (19), in this case $\hat{p}_1 = \hat{p}_2 = \hat{p}$. And,

$$\frac{\hat{p}}{\hat{a}} > 1 \quad \text{iff} \quad e_{12}e_{21} - e_{11}e_{22} - (\eta_{22} - 1)(e_{11} + e_{12}) > 0$$

which, on substitution, is shown to be true; that is, there is now a decrease in p/a—the expenditure required to employ a labour unit—in the new equilibrium.

Now from (14), (15), in this case,

$$\hat{L}_1 = \hat{a} - (\eta_{11} - \eta_{12})\hat{p} = \hat{L}_2 = \hat{a} - (\eta_{22} - \eta_{21})\hat{p},$$

that is,

$$\frac{\hat{L}_1}{\hat{a}} = \frac{\hat{L}_2}{\hat{a}} = 1 - \frac{\hat{p}}{\hat{a}} < 0 \ .$$

In words, labour demand is always increased in both sectors. This is in contrast to the previous two cases where general technical change did not affect labour demand. The difference is due to the fact that in the previous two cases elasticities changed only with changes in relative prices (which are left unchanged by general technical change). In the present case an equiproportionate reduction in prices involves an increase in demand elasticities in the new equilibrium and hence a decrease in p/a, that is, expenditure required to employ a man. With Y fixed this must increase labour demand.

Sector-specific change: $\hat{a}_2 = 0$. Using (18) and (19), with $\hat{a}_2 = 0$, in (14) and (15) we may obtain:

$$\frac{\hat{L}_1}{\hat{a}_1} =$$

$$1 - \frac{\eta_{11}(\eta_{11}-1)(\eta_{22}-1+e_{22}) + \eta_{12}e_{21}(\eta_{11}-1)}{(\eta_{11}-1)(\eta_{22}-1+e_{22})+e_{11}(\eta_{22}-1) + e_{11}e_{22} - e_{12}e_{21}}$$

and

$$\frac{\hat{L_2}}{\hat{a}_1} =$$

$$\frac{(\eta_{11} - 1)[\eta_{22}e_{21} + \eta_{21}(\eta_{22} - 1 + e_{22})]}{(\eta_{11} - 1)(\eta_{22} - 1 + e_{22}) + e_{11}(\eta_{22} - 1) + e_{11}e_{22} - e_{12}e_{21}}$$

It is easily shown that:

it is sufficient for $\dfrac{\hat{L_2}}{\hat{a}_1} \geqslant 0$ that $\eta_{22} \geqslant 2$;

and that $\dfrac{\hat{L_1}}{\hat{a}_1} < 0, \quad \dfrac{\hat{L}}{\hat{a}_1} = \dfrac{\hat{L_1} + \hat{L_2}}{\hat{a}_1} < 0$,

that is, even though sector-specific change affecting sector 1 may reduce labour demand in sector 2, it will always increase labour demand in sector 1 *and* in aggregate.

This is again in contrast to the previous two cases where the *symmetric* equilibrium effect of sector-specific change is to leave total demand unchanged, with demand in sector 2 reduced equiproportionately to the increase in demand in sector *i*.

The main results for the three cases that have been examined are summarized in the next table.

NOTES

1. *See* for example the discussion in Freeman *et al.* (1982) p. 134.
2. 'Technological unemployment' M.Phil. thesis (Oxford, 1980), p. 3. A summary of this work is given in Appendix 1 to this chapter. I only note here that Heffernan assumes that markets are perfectly competitive. This partly justifies the use, in the present chapter, of the (equally strong) assumption that in both sectors output is produced by monopolists or groups of collusive oligopolists (*see* below). Also, in the present chapter, I assume the use of one factor only. Heffernan allows for labour

and capital and is thus able to capture the influence of factor intensities, factor shares and factor substitutability on the relationship between technical change and employment.

3. To provide a unified account of the effect of general and sector-specific technical change the algebra of the following page or so is set out at this point even though it is mostly useful for the examination (in sections 3.3 and 3.4) of the effect of sector-specific change.

4. Marginal revenue for sector 1, say, is $p_1[1 - (1/\eta_{11})]$ whose first derivative with respect to p_1 is $1 - (1/\eta_{11}) + e_{11}/\eta_{11}$ which is positive since $e_{11} = (\eta_{12}\eta_{21}/\eta_{11})$. Marginal revenue is therefore decreasing in output.

5. As noted, for example, by Sinclair (1981, p. 13) technical change may also affect employment by (a) affecting job search; for example microelectronics may reduce deficiencies in, or the cost of, information to the unemployed worker or his potential employer, thus reducing the number of (voluntarily) unemployed job-seekers; and (b) affecting the consumption technology of the household; for example technical change may reduce the amount of time that a household needs to spend out of paid work and leisure and this may induce the household to convert part of the increase in the leisure endowment into extra paid work; 'against this, the households' preferred hours of paid work could drop if technical changes cut the cost of commodity characteristics complementary with leisure' (Sinclair, *ab. cit.* p. 14).

6. Thus the observation of a growing output with stagnant or declining employment levels does not justify questioning 'the ability of western economies to solve their employment problems using ... Keynesian demand stimulation policies' (Rothwell and Zegveld (1981) p. 209 and p.210).

7. The first two terms on the right-hand side of this equation describe consumption by workers, and the third term describes consumption by rentiers. For a derivation of the workers' demand function *see* Weitzman (1982); rentiers are assumed to consume as if a Cobb–Douglas utility function described their preferences.

Table 3.1: *Main results of Chapter 3*

Type of demand function	Type of change		Effect on
	General technical change	Sector-specific technical change	
Constant elasticities	$\dot{L}_1 = \dot{L}_2 = 0$	$\dfrac{\dot{L}_1}{\dot{a}_1} = -\dfrac{\dot{L}_2}{\dot{a}_1}\,;\ \dfrac{\dot{L}}{\dot{a}_1} = 0$	Symmetric equilibrium
		$\dfrac{\dot{L}_1}{\dot{a}_1} = 1 - \eta_{11} < 0;\quad \dfrac{\dot{L}_2}{\dot{a}_1} = \eta_{22} - 1 > 0$	Non-symmetric equilibrium
		$\dfrac{\dot{L}}{\dot{a}_1} = s_{L1}(\eta_{22} - \eta_{11}) + (s_{L2} - s_{L1})(\eta_{22} - 1)$	
CES	$\dot{L}_1 = \dot{L}_2 = 0$	$\dfrac{\dot{L}_1}{\dot{a}_1} = -\dfrac{\dot{L}_2}{\dot{a}_1}\,;\ \dfrac{\dot{L}}{\dot{a}_1} = 0$	Symmetric equilibrium

Non-symmetric equilibrium

$$\frac{\hat{L}}{\hat{a}_1} = \frac{(\eta_{22}-\eta_{11})[\eta_{22}^2+\eta_{11}\eta_{22}+(\eta_{11}-1)(\eta_{22}+\eta_{11})]}{(\eta_{22}+\eta_{11})(\eta_{22}\eta_{11}+\eta_{12}\eta_{11}+\eta_{21}\eta_{22})} \gtreqless 0 \text{ iff } \eta_{22} \gtreqless \eta_{11}$$

$$\frac{\hat{L}_1}{\hat{a}_1} = \frac{\eta_{22}(\eta_{21}-\eta_{11}\eta_{12})}{\eta_{22}\eta_{11}+\eta_{12}\eta_{11}+\eta_{21}\eta_{22}} \gtreqless 0 \text{ iff } \eta_{21} \gtreqless \eta_{11}\eta_{12}$$

$$\frac{\hat{L}_2}{\hat{a}_1} = \frac{\eta_{11}(\eta_{22}\eta_{21}-\eta_{12})}{\eta_{22}\eta_{11}+\eta_{12}\eta_{11}+\eta_{21}\eta_{22}} \gtreqless 0 \text{ iff } \eta_{22}\eta_{21} \gtreqless \eta_{12}$$

Symmetric equilibrium

$$\frac{\hat{L}}{\hat{a}_1} = \frac{\hat{L}_1+\hat{L}_2}{\hat{a}_1} < 0$$

Weitzman-type

$$\frac{\hat{L}_1}{\hat{a}_1}, \frac{\hat{L}_2}{\hat{a}_1} < 0$$

Notation: L_i = labour demand in sector i; L = aggregate labour demand; a_1 = unit labour coefficient in sector 1; η_{ii} = elasticity of demand in sector i; η_{ij} = cross-elasticity of demand; $s_{Li} = L_i/L$.

SECTION B:
PRODUCT INNOVATION

4 Review of Existing Literature and a Preliminary Investigation

4.1 A REVIEW

As noted in the introduction, according to a widely held view the effect of product innovation (as opposed to process innovation) on employment is likely to be favourable. To quote from a recent contribution, 'The way in which the overall demand for labour changes (following the introduction of innovations) depends on the balance between the labour creating effects of new products and the labour displacing effects of process innovations applied to well established products.'[1] In other words, investment which is directed towards the production of new products is thought to have employment-generating effects, while investment devoted to cost-reducing process innovation may tend to reduce aggregate employment.

The view that, unless product innovation takes place, technical change will eventually lead to a reduction in the demand for labour is, usually, based loosely on the argument put forward, and examined in the context of equilibrium growth theory, by Frey in 1969.[2] It relies on the idea that only if the income elasticity of demand is unity will the demand per head for existing products keep pace with the increasing income per head, made possible by process innovation, and that income elasticity is unlikely to be (or remain) equal to unity in the absence of product innovation. To quote Frey:

It can well be said that the introduction of new consumers' products is a necessary condition for economic progress in a market economy. If there were only the same unchanged products available, people would tend to reduce their purchases more and more as they gradually reach satiation. Thus, if there exists an Engel-curve (with an income elasticity of smaller than one, and perhaps even falling over time) for the aggregate of existing products, the consumption ratio of an economy is bound to fall continuously in the absence of new products. With technical progress on the production side, this means that the secularly rising per capita income level is not accompanied by a similarly rising demand. The market system must ultimately break down because of underconsumption.[3]

Statements to the same effect have been produced recently by other authors. For example, in a paper on technological unemployment, Wiles has argued that one of the possible reasons for technological unemployment is that 'consumption is reaching some ceiling of real demand, so that the more productive the labour the less we want of it'. This tendency, he notes, can only be halted by the innovation of new consumer goods.[4] Also, Blattner, in a recent paper on 'Some well-known theoretical propositions on the employment effects of technical change', refers to what he terms 'the saturation problem' and argues that it loses much weight (as a possible reason for technological unemployment) 'insofar as process innovations are combined with product innovation'.[5] Unfortunately, however, no complete analysis of the implications of satiation has ever been offered. Thus, in aggregate neoclassical growth models it is a condition of equilibrium that the consumption ratio remains constant. It is one thing to point out that this condition may not be satisfied unless there is product innovation at a sufficiently rapid rate (as Frey did) and another to explain exactly how the non-satisfaction of this condition leads to a reduction in labour demand, and, even more so, to 'technological unemployment'. To quote another author, a full discussion should *at least* involve 'an examination of the implications of satiated demand on the choices people make between work and leisure':[6] if there simply do not exist 'enough attractive alternatives on which the consumers could spend their incomes ... it can be expected that the supply of labour will be reduced roughly to the level which is justified by the remaining desire for the consumption goods that have to be paid for by money'.[7]

It is because of this that some writers have chosen to stress not that the innovation of new consumer goods prevents satiation of consumption demand, but that consumption demand 'is more responsive to new products than to lower priced old ones (such as purely process innovations would make available)', so that product innovation is more likely to lead to an increase in demand for labour than process innovation (since investment, to satisfy the increased consumption demand, will then be greater).[8]

The view that product (as opposed to process) innovation has employment-generating effects has also emerged in recent discussions on statistical evidence which indicate that the employment-generating effects of new investment were much higher in the 1950s and early 1960s than in the late 1960s and 1970s. It is alleged that this can be explained by the shift in the nature of innovation—a change from product to process innovation—over the period.[9] There is at least some empirical evidence indicating that product innovations leading to the establishment of new industries (such as those introduced in the decade following the Second World War) are usually followed by a lengthy process of standardisation and product improvement, with increasing emphasis being placed on process innovation, as the industries in question mature.[10]

Finally, the idea that product innovation has favourable employment effects, and that it is followed by cost-reducing process innovation, also plays some part in the 'long-wave' theories (originating in the work of Schumpeter), which rely on a link between innovative activity and economic development to explain long-term economic fluctuations.[11] In this respect, one must note the work by Freeman and his collaborators on unemployment and technical innovation (1982). They propound a Schumpeterian view of the long waves—that is, in attempting to explain long-term changes in the magnitude of economic variables, they stress the importance of innovation as 'the main engine of capitalist growth'. Their general argument may be summarised as follows: 'the diffusion of clusters of technical innovations of wide adaptability imparts a substantial upthrust to the growth of the economic system, creating many new opportu-

nities for profitable investment and employment and generating widespread secondary demands for goods and
services'.[12] According to Schumpeter, the first long wave or
Kondratief was based on 'the cluster of textile innovations
and the widespread applications of the steam engine in
manufacturing, the second (on) the railway and steel ... and
the third ... on electricity, the internal combustion engine
and the chemical industry'. The fourth (or, post-war) Kondratief 'could be described as the roughly simultaneous
rolling of several new technology bandwagons; for example,
the computer bandwagon, the television bandwagon, the
transistor bandwagon, the drugs bandwagon and the plastics
bandwagon were all rolling fast in the 1950s as well as some
other bandwagons like consumer durables'.[13]

However, as a new industry or technology matures, several
factors are interacting to reduce the employment generated per
unit of investment. Economies of scale become increasingly important and these work in combination with technical change and
organisational changes associated with increased standardisation.
The profits of innovation are diminished both by competition and
by the pressures on input costs, especially labour costs. A process
of concentration tends to occur and competition forces increasing
attention to the problem of cost-reducing technical change. This
tendency plays an important part in the cyclical movement from
boom to recession.[14]

Note the important part that new capital goods (alongside
new consumer goods) play in the list of innovations that are
supposed to have led to the past Kondratiev upswings.
Remember, however, that in reality the effect of the introduction of a new capital good is very often not so much to
reduce the cost of existing goods but to create the possibility
for the emergence of a whole range of new *consumer* goods
and services. And it is this aspect of capital good innovations
that must be considered by Freeman as mostly responsible
for the expansionary investment associated with the long-
wave upswings. It is certainly true that, as far as the capital
goods mentioned above are concerned, their 'importance'
lies mainly in making possible the introduction of new
consumer goods and services; for example, it is mainly the

car that makes the internal combustion engine 'important', and the radio, television and other consumer durables that make 'important' the developments in valve, transistor and solid-state technology; the same is true to a large extent of the chemical industry. That Freeman *et al.* share the opinion of previously mentioned authors concerning the importance of consumer good innovation is made clear by their remark that 'with rapid income per capita growth it is the development of *new products corresponding to new consumer wants* that is the crucial factor in maintaining the balance between the rate of growth of productivity and the rate of growth of output, and by implication full employment'.[15]

To conclude this section, my aim in this and the next chapter is to try to fill a gap in the existing literature by examining whether any theoretical support can be adduced for the notion that product innovation has positive employment effects. While it is intuitively obvious that the introduction of a new product will create employment opportunities, in the firm or industry concerned, it is less clear whether the *general equilibrium* effect of such an innovation will be positive—bearing in mind the tendency of new products to drive out old ones. Paradoxically, most of the authors of the works mentioned above do not seem to appreciate this or, if they do, they fail to develop a general equilibrium analytical framework for its examination. In a recent work,[16] whilst the author must clearly have a general equilibrium framework in mind when he states that 'The effect of product innovation would be to essentially shift the composition of demand away from all other products to the new' he does not attempt to provide any analysis of the implications of this for the level of employment. Thus, he follows up the above comment, and concludes his discussion, by writing: 'if the new (good) is produced in a less labour intensive way per unit of expenditure than the other products, then aggregate labour demand should fall unless compensation, through for example price changes, increased expenditure, or increased gross investment, acted to reverse the direct impact'. Note, however, that in order to disentangle the 'pure' effect of product innovation one has to assume (as I shall do below) that labour intensity in the production of the new good is the same as that of the existing ones.

In the next section of this chapter I will make clear the mechanism through which product innovation acts on the equilibrium level of employment. This is seen to involve two effects, which I will term the 'welfare effect' and the 'displacement effect' respectively.

4.2 A PRELIMINARY INVESTIGATION WITH PRODUCTS 'HORIZONTALLY' DIFFERENTIATED

The argument of this section is based on a variant of the well-known model of monopolistic competition due to Krugman.[17] (A simple two-good version of the current model was used in section 3.4 above; for convenience, a description of the model, now for n goods, is also given below). I differ from Krugman, firstly in using a slightly different utility function, and further in assuming that the number of firms, n, is exogenously given, each firm being a monopolist who produces one of the n available product varieties (n is assumed to be large). In the present section, I represent product innovation simply as an increase in the parameter n. The limitations of such a view will become apparent later (Chapter 5).

There are N' consumers, N of whom are workers, and the rest rentiers. Rentiers receive all profits. Each worker supplies one unit of labour or none; if he does, he then receives a nominal income of w. Utility from consumption is described by a CES function:

$$V = (C_1^{-\alpha} + C_2^{-\alpha} + \dots + C_n^{-\alpha})^{-1/\alpha}$$

or

$$V = (C_1^{\sigma-1/\sigma} + C_2^{\sigma-1/\sigma} + \dots + C_n^{\sigma-1/\sigma})^{\sigma/\sigma-1};$$

$$\sigma = 1/1+\alpha. \tag{1}$$

Worker j decides whether to work or not depending on whether

$$U_j = V - \omega_j \tag{2}$$

is positive or negative respectively. The parameter ω measures the disutility which worker j gets from work. Thus ω_j is, in effect, the reservation wage of worker j. As before, it is assumed that ω is uniformly distributed over the range $0 \leqslant \omega \leqslant \bar{\omega}$, as shown in Figure 4.1; that is, the density function of ω is

$$g(\omega) = \begin{cases} K & 0 \leqslant \omega \leqslant \bar{\omega} \\ 0 & \text{otherwise} \end{cases}$$

so that $K\bar{\omega} = N$. (It is of course natural, in the present context, to assume simply that the labour supply schedule is upward sloping.)[18].

Finally, we will now assume that one unit of any one of the n (or any new) products can be produced by one unit of labour.

Consider now a consumer receiving income y and maximising utility subject to the budget constraint $y = p_1 C_1 +$

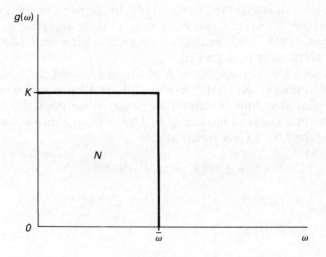

Figure 4.1

$p_2 C_2 + \ldots + p_n C_n$. First-order conditions for maximisation require that

$$\frac{\partial V}{\partial C_i} = \left(\frac{V}{C_i}\right)^{1/\sigma} = \lambda p_i : \quad i = 1, \ldots, n \qquad (3)$$

where λ is the shadow price on the budget constraint. From equations (3) we may obtain:

$$C_i = \frac{y}{p_i^{\sigma}\left[\dfrac{1}{p_1^{\sigma-1}} + \ldots + \dfrac{1}{p_n^{\sigma-1}}\right]} = \frac{y}{p_i^{\sigma} A} \qquad (4)$$

where

$$A = \frac{1}{p_1^{\sigma-1}} + \ldots + \frac{1}{p_n^{\sigma-1}} . \qquad (5)$$

Homotheticity ensures that the composition of the consumption bundle is independent of y. So let C_i^w, C_i^r, represent the consumption of good i of a worker and rentier, respectively. If L workers are in employment, aggregate demand for good i would be

$$X_i = L C_i^w + (N' - N) C_i^r$$

$$= \frac{wL}{p_i^{\sigma} A} + \frac{y(N' - N)}{p_i^{\sigma} A} = \frac{Y}{p_i^{\sigma} A} \qquad (6)$$

where $\quad Y = wL + y(N' - N)$. $\qquad (7)$

From (6) we get the own-price and cross-elasticities of demand, η_d and η_c respectively:

$$\eta_d = -\frac{\partial X_i}{\partial p_i}\frac{p_i}{X_i} = \sigma - (\sigma - 1)\frac{p_i X_i}{Y} \qquad (8)$$

$$\eta_c = \frac{\partial X_i}{\partial p_j}\frac{p_j}{X_i} = (\sigma - 1)\frac{p_j X_i}{Y} . \qquad (9)$$

For a monopolistically competitive equilibrium with positive marginal costs, we must assume that $\sigma > 1$. Equation (9) indicates that the degree of substitutability between the n products will increase with σ.

In a symmetric equilibrium, all firms will charge price p and each will produce output X which will be equal to

$$X = \frac{Y}{p^\sigma A} = \frac{Y}{np} . \tag{10}$$

In this equilibrium,

$$\eta_d = \sigma - [(\sigma - 1)/n] \tag{8'}$$

and $\eta_c = (\sigma - 1)/n$. $\tag{9'}$

Now, from the profit maximisation condition, it is true that $p(1 - 1/\eta_d) = w$, so that the conditions of symmetry and profit maximisation imply that the equilibrium value of the real wage is

$$\left(\frac{w}{p}\right)^* = \frac{(\sigma - 1)\,(n - 1)}{\sigma(n - 1) + 1} \tag{11}[19]$$

In equilibrium, each worker receives $w = pnC^w$. It follows that then $C^w = w/pn$, and taking into account (11),

$$C^{w*} = \frac{(\sigma - 1)\,(n - 1)}{n[\sigma(n - 1) + 1]} . \tag{12}$$

Hence, the utility score V that a worker would obtain from consumption, in equilibrium, were he to supply one unit of labour at wage w, would be (from (1)),

$$[n(C^w)^{\sigma - 1/\sigma}]^{\sigma/\sigma - 1} = \frac{n^{1/\sigma - 1}\,(\sigma - 1)\,(n - 1)}{\sigma(n - 1) + 1} = V^* . \tag{13}$$

Hence, the number of workers offering to work at this equilibrium is equal to the number of workers whose value of ω is less than V^*. The division of the labour force between employed and (voluntarily) unemployed workers is shown in Figure 4.2.

The fraction of the labour force that is willing to work is $L/N = V^*/\bar{\omega}$ and hence, equilibrium employment is

$$L^* = \left(\frac{N}{\bar{\omega}}\right) \frac{n^{1/\sigma-1}\,(\sigma-1)\,(n-1)}{\sigma(n-1)+1} \tag{14}$$

To complete the description of the equilibrium we note that from symmetry and labour market equilibrium $Y/p = nX = L$. From $Y/p = L$ one may obtain the price that firms will need to charge in a symmetric equilibrium to employ L units of labour when nominal aggregate expenditure is given at Y ((11) may then be used to get the equilibrium nominal wage).

From $nX - L$ we may obtain the equilibrium value of X (and y/p). Thus,

$$X^* = \frac{N}{\bar{\omega}} \frac{(\sigma-1)\,(n-1)}{n^{\sigma-2/\sigma-1}\,[\sigma(n-1)+1)]} \ . \tag{15}$$

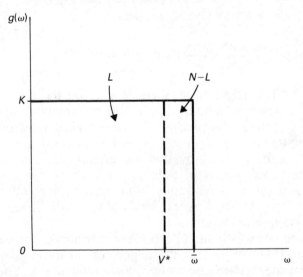

Figure 4.2

Now note that

$$\frac{\partial L^*}{\partial n} = \left(\frac{N}{\bar{\omega}}\right)\frac{\partial V^*}{\partial n} \qquad (16)$$

so that if $\partial V^*/\partial n$ is positive, it is also the case that $\partial L^*/\partial n$ is positive. It may now be easily shown that:

  (ii) An increase in the number of products, n, will, *ceteris paribus*, lead to an increase in the equilibrium value of the workers' utility score, V, and hence to an increase in the amount of labour employed in equilibrium; that is,

$$\frac{\partial V^*}{\partial n} > 0 \Rightarrow \frac{\partial L^*}{\partial n} > 0 . \qquad (17)$$

  (ii) The increase in the equilibrium supply of labour and employment as n increases, diminishes with the degree of substitutability between the products σ; that is,

$$\frac{\partial}{\partial \sigma}\left(\frac{\partial V^*}{\partial n}\right) < 0 \Rightarrow \frac{\partial}{\partial n}\left(\frac{\partial L^*}{\partial n}\right) < 0 . \qquad (18)[20]$$

  (iii) $\quad \dfrac{\partial V^*}{\partial n}, \dfrac{\partial L^*}{\partial n} \to 0$ as $\sigma \to \infty$. $\qquad (19)$

  The effect of an increase in n on the equilibrium level of labour supply and employment tends to zero as the products become perfect substitutes.

Inequality (17) expresses what I shall term the *welfare effect* of product innovation on employment: given the degree of substitutability, the appearance of new products increases the workers' utility from consumption, relative to their disutility from work, and this in turn leads to an increase in employment.

Inequalities (18) and (19) on the other hand, suggest that: (from (18)) the greater the degree of substitutability, the smaller the welfare effect of product innovation will be, and (from (19)) that for large enough σ this effect will be

negligible. This is the result of new products simply displacing old ones as substitutability between them increases—and
this goes hand in hand, moreover, with the fact that such
introductions do not much affect the consumer's welfare.
For this reason, we shall say that (18) and (19) reflect the
displacement effect of product innovation on employment.
To further clarify this latter effect, I will now consider how
the equilibrium output of each monopolist changes as new
products are introduced. It is easily seen from (15) that,

(iv) $\dfrac{\partial X^*}{\partial n} > 0$ for $1 < \sigma \leqslant 2$

and, for sufficiently large n,

$$\frac{\partial X^*}{\partial n} < 0 \quad \text{for} \quad \sigma > 2 \ .$$

That is, as σ increases beyond 2 the introduction of new
products will tend to reduce the equilibrium level of output
of each monopolist.

The present model is not general enough to tell the full
story. It does suggest, however, that, were a new product to
displace an old one completely, its introduction might have
no effect on welfare and hence on employment. This is
intuitively plausible when we think of a world in which
products are 'horizontally' differentiated, as is the case in
the above (Chamberlinian-type) model of monopolistic
competition. However, in many industries (for example in
those producing consumer durables) products are differentiated 'vertically'; that is, by quality. In this case product
innovation is associated with the introduction of a new,
higher quality alternative to existing products. The question
is whether or not it is still the case that, by displacing an old
quality, the introduction of a new quality will have no effect
on utility and the equilibrium level of employment. Such
concerns are relevant not only in the immediately obvious
setting in which one generation of computers is replaced by
the next; they are also germane to the larger 'Schumpeterian' scenario in which, for example, the thriving Coventry

bicycle industry gave way in the pre-war years to the growing car industry. They are the subject of the analysis of Chapter 5.

4.3 PRODUCT INNOVATION: SHORT RUN VERSUS LONG RUN

It is important, at this point, to relate the preceding discussion to our main theme, which is concerned with the distinction between process and product innovation as regards their effect on the equilibrium level of employment. *What the above discussion shows is that, in contrast to process innovation, the impact effect of which may be to reduce the equilibrium level of employment (as indicated in Chapter 3), the impact effect of product innovation cannot be unfavourable (and it is likely to be positive).* This conclusion is reinforced by the analysis of Chapter 5.

On the other hand, as in the previous chapter, in the present setting, *short-run* difficulties would arise in attaining the new equilibrium as a result of (downward) nominal wage rigidities. To clarify this point we note that, from the symmetry condition (10) and equation (11),

$$nX = \frac{Y}{p} = \frac{Y}{w} \left[\frac{(n-1)(\sigma-1)}{\sigma(n-1)+1} \right] .$$

On the other hand, labour supply is, from (14),

$$L = \frac{N}{\bar{\omega}} V = \frac{N}{\bar{\omega}} n^{1/\sigma-1} \left[\frac{(n-1)(\sigma-1)}{\sigma(n-1)+1} \right] .$$

Hence, to attain the new equilibrium, where $nX = L$, following an increase in n, the nominal wage must be reduced. So, if the nominal wage is sticky in the short run, product innovation will result in an excess supply of labour.

APPENDIX

Proof of Equation (18):
From (13) in Chapter 4,

$$\frac{\partial V^*}{\partial \sigma} = \frac{V^*}{(\sigma - 1)^2}\left[\frac{n(\sigma - 1)}{\sigma(n - 1) + 1} - \log n\right] \qquad \text{(A)}$$

(A) is negative if $z(n,\sigma) = [n(\sigma - 1)]/[\sigma(n - 1) + 1] < \log n$.

Now

$$\frac{\partial z(n,\sigma)}{\partial \sigma} > 0 \qquad \text{(B)}$$

so that, $z(n,\sigma)$ is monotonically increasing in σ. Further, by considering $\sigma = 1 + \epsilon$, where ϵ is a positive number, we can show that

$$0 < \frac{n(\sigma - 1)}{\sigma(n - 1) + 1} < \frac{n}{n - 1} . \qquad \text{(C)}$$

It is sufficient for

$$n/(n - 1) < \log n \qquad \text{(D)}$$

that $n \geqslant 4$. From (B), (C) and (D) it follows that for all n greater than or equal to 4 and σ greater than one $[n(\sigma - 1)]/[\sigma(n - 1) + 1] < \log n$.

Since we have assumed n to be large, this implies that

$$\frac{\partial V^*}{\partial \sigma} < 0 . \qquad \text{(E)}$$

And since, from (13),

$$\frac{\partial V^*}{\partial n} = V^*\left[\frac{n\sigma - 1}{n(n - 1)(\sigma - 1)} - \frac{\sigma}{\sigma(n - 1) + 1}\right]$$

it is easily seen that (E) is sufficient for

$$\frac{\partial}{\partial \sigma}\left(\frac{\partial V^*}{\partial n}\right) < 0 \ .$$

NOTES

1. Williams, B. (1983a), p. 5. See also Williams, B. (1983b), and Stoneman, P. (1984), p. 61–63 and p. 69.
2. Frey (1969), p. 29.
3. Presumably, Frey and some other authors to be mentioned below will *explain* the long-run constancy in the propensity to consume by pointing to the quite steady introduction of new goods and new qualities over the past 200 years. Hence, it does not seem proper to try to refute the satiation argument by noting the constancy in the propensity to consume, as some authors have done recently (e.g., Clark and Cooper (1982), p. 28).
4. Wiles (1983), p. 6.
5. Blattner (1979), pp. 65–6.
6. Clark and Cooper, *ab. cit.*, p. 28.
7. Blattner (1983), p. 64.
8. Clark and Cooper, *ab. cit.*, p. 29; they argue that product innovation may lead to more rapid scrapping in long-lived consumer durables.
9. Rothwell and Zegveld (1981), pp. 220–2; they use data for West Germany and Great Britain.
10. *See* Abernathy and Utterback (1978); especially, pp. 44–7.
11. *See*, for example, Freeman *et al.* (1982), p. 75.
12. These 'clusters' of innovations are associated 'with a technological web, with the growth of new industries and services involving distinct new groupings of firms with their own subculture and distinct technology and with new patterns of consumer behaviour', p. 68.
13. Freeman *et al.*, *ab. cit.*, pp. 67–8.
14. Freeman *et al.*, *ab. cit.*, p. 75.
15. Freeman *et al.*, *ab. cit.*, p. 141; the emphasis is mine.
16. Stoneman (1983), p. 181.
17. Krugman (1979); this is, in turn, a special case of the model by Dixit and Stiglitz (1977).

18. This is not to deny that ongoing product innovation, that increases workers' utility scores from consumption, is consistent in the long run with constant, or falling, hours of work. As mentioned at the beginning of this chapter and in the introduction, the context of the literature under discussion here is that process innovation may lead to a reduction in employment and product innovation may (perhaps partly) offset this. For evidence indicating a 25 per cent reduction in hours per year of full-time British male workers, between 1890 and 1975, see Williams (1983a), p. 6.

19. Note that w/p is increasing in σ and n, the degree of substitutability between and the number of products. This is the effect of increased competition as σ and n increases; indeed, in the limit as $\sigma \to \infty \Rightarrow w \to p$, that is, the equilibrium tends to zero-profit equilibrium. On the other hand, whilst for given σ an increase in n leads to an increase in competition and the equilibrium real wage, profits here will remain positive, for any n. Salop and Perloff (1985) give conditions that ensure that price will tend to marginal cost as n increases.

20. See Appendix to Chapter 4 for proof.

5 Product Innovation Reconsidered

5.1 AN ALTERNATIVE MODEL: THE 'VERTICAL' DIFFERENTIATION CASE

5.1.1 Introduction: Price Equilibrium in Industries with Products 'Vertically' Differentiated

The central theorem of the 'vertical differentiation' literature states that, if *variable* cost does not increase too rapidly, as quality is increased, then the following 'finiteness' property holds (Shaked and Sutton, 1983a):

there will exist, an upper bound, independent of product qualities, to the number of firms which can survive with positive market shares, and prices in excess of unit variable cost, at a Nash equilibrium in prices.

This arises as follows:

whatever the set of products entered, competition between certain surviving products drives their prices down to a level where every consumer prefers either to make no purchase, or to buy one of these surviving goods at its equilibrium price, rather than switch to any of the excluded products, at any price sufficient to cover unit variable cost (Shaked and Sutton, *op. cit.*).

Such an outcome depends, as noted, on the fact that unit variable cost does not increase too rapidly with increases in quality; this is likely to hold in those industries where the

80

main burden of quality improvement takes the form of research and development (R and D) or other fixed costs. Our present case, in which unit variable cost will be assumed constant over all qualities, is a special case of this. The situation where the finiteness property holds has been labelled a 'Natural Oligopoly' (Shaked and Sutton, *op. cit.*).

In the present section I discuss price equilibrium in an industry where products are 'vertically' differentiated. I follow recent expositions of the 'Natural Oligopoly' model,[1] relying mainly on the simplest version of that model. Then, in section 5.2, I will consider product innovation using a general equilibrium model (developed in 5.1.2. below) with one industry 'vertically' differentiated.

Assume that there are n firms in the quality good industry and that they sell to N consumers. Each of the latter buys one unit of one (or possibly none) of the qualities on offer. The consumers' distribution of income (e) is described by a uniform density taking the value s on some support (a,b), where $a > 0$. All consumers have the same utility function as follows: a consumer of income e obtains a utility score given by $u_i(e - p_i)$ from consuming one unit of product i, and spending his remaining income on 'other things'. His utility score is $u_0 e$ if he does not purchase any of the quality goods, where $u_0 < u_1 < u_2 < ... < u_n$, that is, I label goods in increasing order of quality.

Now note that for price p_k charged by the firms producing quality k and p_{k-1} charged by firms producing $k-1$, we may define income e_k that satisfies

$$u_k(e - p_k) = u_{k-1}(e - p_{k-1}), \tag{1}$$

that is, e_k is the income level that would make a consumer indifferent between consuming k at price p_k and $k - 1$ at price p_{k-1}. Hence, a consumer of income greater than e_k, will strictly prefer good k at price p_k to good $k - 1$ at price p_{k-1}: and so, at any given prices, we may partition consumers into the respective market shares of successive firms. Firm n will sell to all those with income between b and e_n, firm $n - 1$ to those of income e_n to e_{n-1}, and so on. From this one may write down the demand schedule faced by any firm that will depend on the qualities, and the prices offered by its neighbours.

Consider the demand schedule faced by firm n, which offers the top quality product. Suppose to begin with, that its neighbour offers a product of quality u_{n-1} at price c, which equals its unit variable cost.[2] The price of quality good n that would make a worker of income e indifferent between consuming a unit of this and a unit of quality good $n - 1$, offered at c, is given by

$$u_n(e - p_n) = u_{n-1}(e - c), \qquad (1')$$

that is, as should be obvious from the fact that a worker's utility score is increasing in quality, this price is greater than $c = p_{n-1}$ and given by $p_n = [(u_n - u_{n-1})/u_n] \, e + (u_{n-1}/u_n) \, c$, that is, it is increasing in income. Let the richest worker, of income $e = b$, be willing to pay price $\hat{p}_n > p_{n-1} = c$ in order to consume (the higher quality) good n, rather than good $n - 1$; this determines the vertical intercept of the demand schedule (Figure 5.1). As poorer workers are willing to pay less, demand increases as price falls, until that price is reached at which the poorest worker (worker of income $e = a$) is just willing to pay for good n, rather than consume good $n - 1$ at price c. Let this price (that satisfies $u_n \, (a - p_n) = u_{n-1}(a - c)$) be $\bar{p}_n$ (Figure 5.1).

Now if the lower quality firm $n - 1$ instead sets some price greater than c then the demand schedule of the firm producing quality n simply shifts upwards. As is readily checked, moreover, from inspection of $(1')$ above, these demand schedules are linear.[3]

From $(1')$, the vertical intercept of the demand schedule of firm n, when $n - 1$ is offered at c, is

$$\hat{p}_n = [(u_n - u_{n-1})/u_n] \, b + (u_{n-1}/u_n)c,$$

that is, the price a worker of income $e = b$ is prepared to pay to consume n, rather than $n - 1$. Now the profit-maximising price of a firm facing a linear demand schedule and constant unit cost, is equal to the unit cost plus half the difference

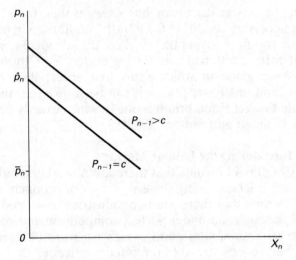

Figure 5.1

between the vertical intercept and the unit cost. Hence, here the profit maximising price p_n^* would be

$$p_n^* = c + \tfrac{1}{2}\{[(u_n - u_{n-1})/u_n]\,(b - c)\}$$

unless this is less than

$$\bar{p}_n = [(u_n - u_{n-1})/u_n]\,a + (u_{n-1}/u_n)c.$$

p_n^* is less than $\bar{p}_n$ if $a > (b + c)/2$, that is, if the range of incomes is sufficiently narrow. With $a > (b + c)/2$, we have a corner solution—the firm producing n sets a price $\bar{p}_n$ and covers the market, with firm $n - 1$ obtaining a zero market share. This represents the most extreme possibility, in which the industry is a 'Natural Monopoly'. It is on this case that I focus below. (If the range of incomes is broader, so that $a < (b + c)/2$, it can be shown that firm n will not cover the market. However, if $a > (b + c)/4$, then the market will be covered by the top two firms, and so on; Shaked and Sutton, 1983a.)

What the above discussion has shown is that, for $a > (b + c)/2$, a necessary condition for a Nash equilibrium in prices is that the top firm covers the market. By introducing a fixed cost of entry $\epsilon > 0$, and considering Perfect Equilibrium in a three-stage game in which firms first enter, then choose quality, and finally set prices, it can be shown that the only possible Perfect Equilibrium is one in which exactly one firm enters (Shaked and Sutton, 1982).

5.1.2 Introducing the Labour Market
As in Chapter 4 I assume that there are N workers (indexed $j = 1, \ldots N$), labour being the only factor of production. But now I assume that there are two industries: one produces a homogeneous good under perfect competition and constant returns (the numeraire good, which we will call 'corn'); in the other, goods are differentiated vertically, that is, by quality, with each firm producing one product (quality level). All profit goes to rentiers, who spend it all on 'corn'. Each worker buys one unit of some one of the quality goods (or none), spending the rest of his income on 'corn'. Since the latter is produced under perfect competition with constant returns to scale, it follows that, in equilibrium, a worker receives a wage in terms of corn which equals the amount of corn which he can produce. I assume that workers differ in their marginal product in terms of corn, which we denote as e (efficiency).

Worker j's preferences will be described by a function of the form

$$U_j = U(f_j \, (i, \, x) - \omega_j) \tag{2}$$

where f_j, the utility score of worker j, is an increasing function of i and x ; i is the index of quality. The amount of corn consumed is denoted by x, and ω_j measures the disutility of work for worker j.

Let the efficiency of worker j, e_j, indicate the number of units of corn worker j can produce per period, and assume that e is distributed over a range $0 < a \leqslant e \leqslant b$. So, we can denote worker's income, in terms of corn, ranging from a to b, by e. The amount of corn consumed by a worker of efficiency e who does not purchase a quality good is, of course, e, and if he consumes good i his consumption of corn is $e - p_i$ (p_i being the price of good i, expressed in terms of corn). So, since x equals either e or $e - p_i$, I will write the worker's utility score $f(i,x)$ for any given p_i, as

$$f(i,e) = \max [u_0 e, u_i(e - p_i)]; \quad i = 1, \ldots, n \qquad (3)$$

where as already noted $u_0 < u_1 < u_2 < \ldots < u_n$.

Assume that $\bar{\omega}$, which here indicates the disutility of work expressed per unit of output produced,[4] is distributed over the range $0 \leqslant \omega \leqslant \bar{\omega}$, so that e and ω are uniformly distributed with $g(e,\omega) = 1$ on $0 \leqslant \omega \leqslant \bar{\omega}$ and $0 < a \leqslant e \leqslant b$, as shown in Figure 5.2.

I assume that (2) takes the following form:

$$U_j = f_j(i, e_j) - \omega_j e_j; \quad i = 1, \ldots, n: \quad j = 1, \ldots, N \quad (2')$$

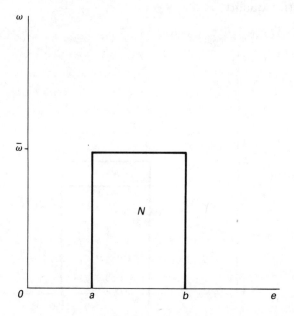

Figure 5.2

so that j works if $f_j(i, e_j) > \omega_j e_j$ and remains unemployed otherwise.

When there are no quality goods, $f_j(i, e_j) = u_0 e_j$ and then, from (2')

$$U_j = u_0 e_j - \omega_j e_j = (u_0 - \omega_j)e_j \tag{4}$$

so that j would remain unemployed if $\omega_j > u_0$. In Figure 5.3, $\omega^* = u_0$ and workers with $\omega < \omega^*$ would be employed (in the absence of quality goods). Employment is indicated by L.

5.2 PRODUCT INNOVATION AGAIN

In the present section I will use the model described in section 5.1 to examine the effect on employment of the introduction of a new quality good. I first assume that only the outside good is available. I then turn to the analysis of product innovation by considering the introduction of a superior quality.

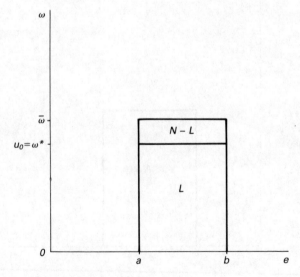

Figure 5.3

To start with, assume that there is no quality good available and then introduce good of quality u_k. One must first describe the conditions under which u_k will cover the quality good market. To this effect, I start by assuming the existence of two quality goods, u_1 and u_2, where $u_1 < u_2$, together with the outside good (good 0); I proceed to analyse the conditions under which, in price equilibrium, u_2 will cover the market. The general equilibrium character of the present model leads to some modifications in the analysis of the 'vertically' differentiated industry presented in the previous section.

The utility score, $f(i,e)$, of a worker of income e is now given by (3) above, with $i = 1,2$, that is,

$$f(i,e) = \max[u_0 e, u_i(e - p_i)] ; \quad i = 1,2 . \tag{5}$$

The worker's utility is described by

$$U = f(i,e) - \omega e$$

or $\quad U = \max[u_0 e, u_i(e - p_i)] - \omega e ; \quad i = 1,2 . \tag{6}$

Assume now that u_1 is priced at its unit cost c and then consider the following equations, from (6):

First, $\quad \omega e = u_2(e - p_2) \Rightarrow \omega = u_2(1 - p_2/e) . \tag{7}$

Then, $\quad \omega e = u_1(e - c) \Rightarrow \omega = u_1(1 - c/e) \tag{8}$

and $\quad \omega e = u_0 e \Rightarrow \omega = u_0 . \tag{9}$

In Figure 5.4, (7), (8) and (9) have been drawn as *AB, CD* and *HL* ('horizontal line'), respectively.
At given p_2, (7) gives combinations of ω and e for which workers are indifferent between staying unemployed and working and consuming a unit of u_2; at given p_1, $(p_1 = c)$, (8) gives combinations of ω and e for which workers are indifferent between staying unemployed and working and consuming a unit of u_1. Finally, from (9), those of $\omega > u_0$

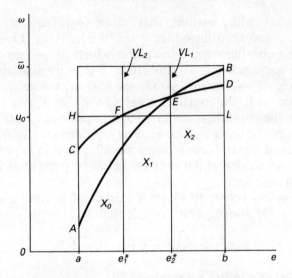

Figure 5.4:   *Exployment* = $X_0 + X_1 + X_2$

prefer staying unemployed rather than working and consuming just 'corn'.

Now AB and CD intersect at the income level that would make a worker indifferent between a unit of u_2 and a unit of u_1 offered at p_2 ($>c$) and c, respectively, that is, at income level e_2^*,

$$e_2^* = [u_2/(u_2 - u_1)]p_2 - [u_1/(u_2 - u_1)]c \qquad (10)$$

that satisfies

$$u_1(e - c) = u_2(e - p_2) ; \qquad (10')$$

whilst CD and HL intersect at the income level, e_1^*, that would make a worker indifferent between a unit of u_1 offered at c and spending all income on corn, that is,

$$e_1^* = [u_1/(u_1 - u_0)]c \qquad (11)$$

satisfies

$$u_0 e = u_1(e - c) \tag{11'}$$

I assume, in Figure 5.4, that p_2 is large enough to make $e_2^* > e_1^*$ so that point E is above HL as indicated.

Now, it is clear from (10') that workers with income $e > e_2^*$ will strictly prefer u_2 to u_1 when priced at p_2 ($>c$) and c, respectively. Of these workers, those with ωs beneath AB obtain employment. Hence, at these prices, demand for u_2, X_2, is $X_2 =$ area (BEe_2^*b).

From (11') workers with income $e > e_1^*$ will strictly prefer u_1 (priced at c) to 'all corn'; of these workers, those with ωs beneath CD obtain employment. Hence, demand for u_1, X_1, at these prices is $X_1 =$ area $(EFe_1^*e_2^*)$.

Finally workers with $e > e_1^*$ will strictly prefer 'all corn' to u_1 priced at c and, of these workers, those with ωs beneath HL obtain employment— this area I label X_0 in Figure 5.4. Aggregate employment, L, at these prices, will be, therefore, $L =$ area $(BEFHab) = X_0 + X_1 + X_2$.

Now, from (7), as p_2 is reduced AB shifts upwards, and, from (10), as p_2 is reduced, VL_1 shifts to the left. Both these movements lead to an increase in the demand for u_2, as previously unemployed workers enter employment and consume u_2, and workers previously consuming u_1 now choose u_2. In Figure 5.5 I illustrate this (the old situation is shown by dotted curves AB, CD, VL_1 and VL_2).

As p_2 is reduced, AB shifts to $A'B'$ and demand for u_2 increases from BEe_2^*b to $B'Fe_1^*b$ (with VL_1 coinciding with VL_2); at this level of p_2, say p_2', demand for u_1 (priced at c) drops to zero (demand for the outside good remains unaffected, equal to $FHae_1^*$). However, for p_2 less than p_2', as no workers demand u_1 any more, VL_1 is not defined by (10) but rather by

$$\hat{e}_2^* = [u_2/(u_2 - u_0)]p_2, \tag{12}$$

that is, by the level of e satisfying

$$u_0 e = u_2(e - p_2) \tag{12'}$$

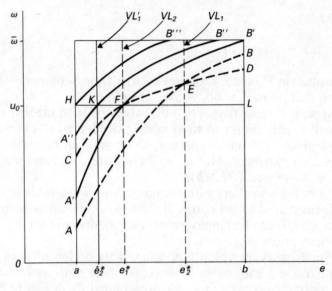

Figure 5.5

(this makes a worker indifferent between the outside good and a unit of u_2 with $e - p_2$ spent on the outside good). This implies that a given proportionate reduction in p_2 shifts VL_1 to the left less for $p_2 \leqslant p_2'$ than for $p_2 > p_2'$, that is, such a reduction increases demand for u_2 more rapidly for $p_2 > p_2'$ than for $p_2 \leqslant p_2'$. Hence, at $p_2 = p_2'$, demand for u_2 has a kink, as shown in Figure 5.6.

A further reduction in p_2, to a level below p_2', shifts $A'B'$ to $A''B''$ (Figure 5.5), and demand for u_2 increases to $B''k$ $\hat{e}_2^* b$. Let $\bar{p}_2$ be the price at which AB becomes HB''' (Figure 5.5), that is, at which (7) (that defines the AB curves) intersects HL at point H with the vertical line, defined by (12), coinciding with the one originating at $e = a$. From (12) $\bar{p}_2$ is equal to $[(u_2 - u_0)/u_2]a$. At $\bar{p}_2$ demand for u_2 is $B'''Hab$ (Figure 5.5). There can be no further shift to the left of the vertical line as p_2 is reduced below $\bar{p}_2$ (*all* workers in employment choose to consume u_2 when it is priced at $\bar{p}_2$), even though, of course, HB''' shifts upwards (workers previously unemployed enter employment and consume u_2).

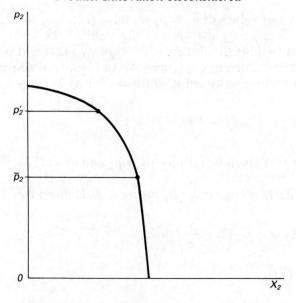

Figure 5.6

Thus (as will also be explained more formally below) there is, at $\bar{p}_2$, another kink in the demand schedule for u_2 (also shown in Figure 5.6).

We may now obtain the conditions under which u_2 will cover the quality good market. Profit from sales of u_2 is

$$\Pi_2 = (p_2 - c)X_2$$

so that

$$\frac{d\Pi_2}{dp_2} = X_2(1 - \eta) - c \frac{dX_2}{dp_2}$$

where $\eta = - (dX_2/dp_2) (p_2/X_2)$. Hence $d\Pi_2/dp_2$ is negative for as long as η remains sufficiently greater than unity. Since at $\bar{p}_2$ all workers in employment choose to consume u_2, for u_2 to cover the market it is sufficient that $d\Pi_2/dp_2$ is negative on the left of the kink associated with $\bar{p}_2$ but not so on the right of this kink.

Now, for values of $p_2 \geqslant \bar{p}_2$ we have seen that the demand for u_2 is given by the area to the right of the vertical line defined by (10) (or, for $\bar{p}_2 \leqslant p_2 < p_2'$ by (12)) and beneath the curve defined by (7) (curve AB in Figure 5.4 above). We may therefore write demand for u_2, for $p_2 \geqslant \bar{p}_2$ as

$$X_2 = \int_{e^*}^{b} u_2\left(1 - \frac{p_2}{e}\right)de \tag{13}$$

where e^* is given by (10) for $p_2 \geqslant p_2'$ and by (12) for $\bar{p}_2 \leqslant p_2 < p_2'$.

Similarly, demand for u_2 for $p_2 < \bar{p}_2$ is given by

$$X_2 = \int_{a}^{b} u_2\left(1 - \frac{p_2}{e}\right)de \ . \tag{14}$$

From (13),

$$X_2 = u_2(b - e^*) - u_2 p_2 \log_e\left(\frac{b}{e^*}\right) \tag{13'}$$

for $p_2 \geqslant \bar{p}_2$. And from (14),

$$X_2 = u_2(b - a) - u_2 p_2 \log_e\left(\frac{b}{a}\right) \tag{14'}$$

for $p_2 < \bar{p}_2$. (Hence for $p_2 < \bar{p}_2$ the demand schedule for u_2 is linear).

Also from (13), for $p_2 \geqslant \bar{p}_2$,

$$\frac{dX_2}{dp_2} = -\frac{de^*}{dp_2} u_2\left(1 - \frac{p_2}{e^*}\right) + \int_{e^*}^{b}\left\{\frac{d}{dp_2}\left[u_2\left(1 - \frac{p_2}{e}\right)\right]\right\}de \tag{15}$$

$$= -\frac{de^*}{dp_2} u_2\left(1 - \frac{p_2}{e^*}\right) - u_2 \log_e\left(\frac{b}{e^*}\right) \tag{15'}$$

and from (14), for $p_2 < \bar{p}_2$,

$$\frac{dX_2}{dp_2} = \int_{a}^{b}\left\{\frac{d}{dp_2}\left[u_2\left(1 - \frac{p_2}{e}\right)\right]\right\}de = -u_2 \log_e\left(\frac{b}{a}\right) \tag{16}$$

(Notice that the kink associated with p_2' (figure 5.6) can be explained by differentiating (15') with respect to p_2 and by comparing the resulting expression for the case where e^* is given by (10) and the case where e^* is given by (12). Also, since $de^*/dp_2 > 0$ in (15'), comparison of (15') and (16) explains the kink associated with $\bar{p}_2$ in Figure 5.6.)

In the appendix to this chapter I show that there is a range of values of a, sufficiently close to b, that makes η sufficiently greater than unity and thus $d\pi_2/dp_2 < 0$ to the left of the kink associated with $\bar{p}_2$ and also makes $d\pi_2/dp_2 > 0$ to the right of this kink. Assuming that the income distribution satisfies this condition, in price equilibrium following the introduction of u_2, this good will cover the quality good market at a price $p_2 = \bar{p}_2 = [(u_2 - u_0)/u_2]a$, that is, the price that makes workers of income a indifferent between spending all income on the outside good and consuming one unit of u_2 with $a - p_2$ of the outside good.

From Figure 5.5, at this equilibrium X_2 = area ($B'''\,Hab$) = L = employment.

The change in employment, following the introduction of u_2, is also indicated in Figure 5.7 below by ΔL.

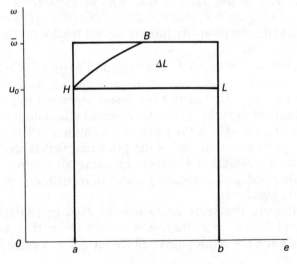

Figure 5.7

We now turn to the analysis of product innovation, by considering the introduction of a good of superior quality u_3. We proceed in two steps. First, we consider the 'comparative static' exercise in which the quality of the monopolist's product increases to u_3.[5] Secondly, we consider the case where a new firm offers the superior quality.

In the first case, curve AB in Figure 5.4 will be defined by

$$\omega = u_3 \left[1 - (p_3/e)\right] \tag{17}$$

(which replaces equation (7)), and VL_1 will now be given by

$$e_3^* = \frac{u_3}{u_3 - u_1} p_3 - \frac{u_1}{u_3 - u_1} c , \tag{18}$$

that is, by the level of income satisfying

$$u_1(e - c) = u_3(e - p_3) \tag{18'}$$

((18) – (18′) replacing (10) and (10′)). That is, at given prices, an increase in quality of the good offered by the monopolist leads to a shift upwards of curve AB and a shift to the left of the vertical line VL_1 in Figure 5.4. This is shown in Figure 5.8 where $A'B'$ is defined by (17) and VL_1' by (18) (the original situation is shown by dotted lines AB, CD, VL_1 and VL_2).

The shift in AB and VL_1 illustrated in Figure 5.8 implies a shift in the demand curve of the monopolist, as depicted in Figure 5.9 (for simplicity I use linear segments to represent the demand curves). D_2 is the demand schedule for u_2 and D_3 for u_3; $p_3'(>p_2')$ is the price at which the market share of u_1 drops to zero; $\bar{p}_3(>\bar{p}_2)$ is the price that makes workers of income a indifferent between spending all income on the outside good and consuming a unit of u_3 with $a - p_3$ of the outside good.

Following the same procedure as used in analysing the demand for u_2 one may now easily show that in price equilibrium the monopolist will charge for u_3 a price $p_3 = \bar{p}_3$ given by

$$\bar{p}_3 = [(u_3 - u_0)/u_3]a, \tag{19}$$

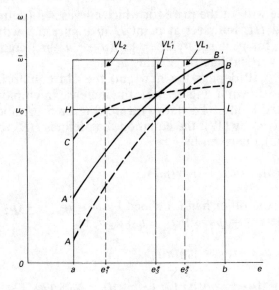

Figure 5.8

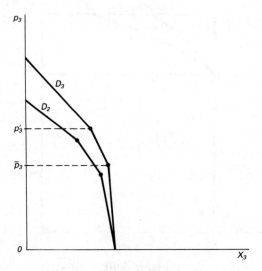

Figure 5.9

that is, he will set the price for which curves AB (defined by (17)) and HL intersect at point H in Figure 5.8 with VL'_1 (defined, for $p < p'_3$, by $e^*_3 = [u_3/(u_3 - u_0)]p_3$) coinciding with the vertical line originating at a.

Figure 5.10 depicts the new and the old equilibria (the latter was shown in Figure 5.7); the increase in employment is indicated by ΔL. To clarify further Figure 5.10, note that with p_3 given by (19), the equation that defines HB' ($\omega = u_3 [1 - (p_3/e)]$) is given by

$$\omega = u_3 - (u_3 - u_0)\,(a/e) \,. \tag{20}$$

HB on the other hand, defined by $\omega = u_2 [1 - (p_2/e)]$, is given when $p_2 = \bar{p}_2 = [(u_2 - u_0)/u_2]a$, by

$$\omega = u_2 - (u_2 - u_0)(a/e) \tag{20'}$$

Since $u_3 - (u_3 - u_0)(a/e) > u_2 - (u_2 - u_0)(a/e)$

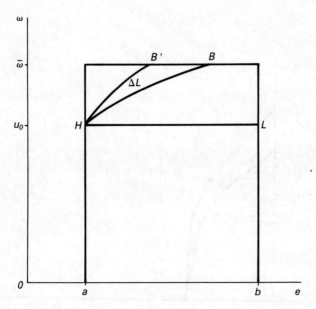

Figure 5.10

HB' lies wholly above *HB* for all $e > a$. This explains the increase in employment as depicted in Figure 5.10.[6]

Let us now finally assume that a new improved quality (u_3) is introduced by a new firm (rather than the monopolist producing u_2). We shall show that in this case the resulting increase in the equilibrium level of employment is greater than the increase resulting when the existing firm introduces u_3—the case examined above.

When u_3 is introduced by a new firm the curve giving combinations of ω and e that makes workers indifferent between staying unemployed, and working and consuming u_3, will again be defined by (17), that is, as when the existing monopolist introduces u_3. On the other hand, now, price competition between the two firms implies that in equilibrium the price of the existing monopolist is reduced from $\bar{p}_2$ to c. Figure 5.11 reproduces Figure 5.7 (illustrating the old

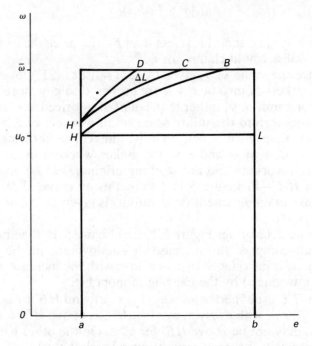

Figure 5.11

equilibrium) with HB shifting to $H'C$ when p_2 is reduced to c: HB is defined by $\omega = u_2\,[1 - (\bar{p}_2/e)]$ and $H'C$ by $\omega = u_2[1 - (c/e)]$.

The vertical line defined by the level of income at which workers are indifferent between u_2 and u_3 will in this case be given by

$$e_3^* = [u_3/(u_3 - u_2)]p_3 - [u_2/(u_3 - u_2)]c, \qquad (21)$$

that is, by the level of income satisfying

$$u_2(e - c) = u_3(e - p_3). \qquad (21')^7$$

Again, the previous analysis suggests that in equilibrium the new firm will charge a price such that workers of income a are indifferent between a unit of u_2 priced at c and a unit of u_3, that is, from (21'), it will charge $p_3 = p_3^n$ where

$$p_3^n = [(u_3 - u_2)/u_3]a + (u_2/u_3)c \; . \qquad (22)$$

It is easily seen that this is less than $\bar{p}_3$, the price the existing monopolist would charge for u_3.[8]

Since the value of p_3 given by (22) satisfies (21') for $e = a$ and workers of income $e > a$ are prepared to pay more than that for a unit of u_3 rather than a unit of u_2 priced at c, in the new equilibrium the utility score of all workers of $e > a$ is greater than $u_2(e - c)$, that is, the curve showing the combination of ω and e which makes workers indifferent between working and not working originates at H' and lies above $H'C$—in Figure 5.11 I show this by curve $H'D$. The increase in employment (and output) is given by $\Delta L =$ area $(BD\,H'H)$.

Figure 5.12 brings Figure 5.10 and Figure 5.11 together so we can compare the increase in employment in the case where u_3 is introduced by a new firm with the increase when u_3 is introduced by the existing monopolist.

Since $H'C$ is defined by $\omega = u_2\,[1 - (c/e)]$ and HB' by $\omega = u_3\,[1 - (\bar{p}_3/e)]$, with $\bar{p}_3$ given by (19), $H'C$ is above HB' for $e = a$, but may not be above HB' for all e. On the other hand, a new firm will charge in equilibrium p_3^n such that $p_3^n < \bar{p}_3$, with

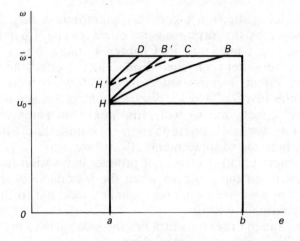

Figure 5.12

$H'D$ defined by $\omega = u_3 [1 - (p_3^n/e)]$. Hence $H'D$ lies wholly above HB' so that, as indicated in Figure 5.12, area $(BDH'H) >$ area $(BB'H)$, that is, the increase in employment is greatest when u_3 is introduced by a new firm rather than the existing monopolist.

Thus, we have shown that the employment-generating effect of the new innovation is enhanced in so far as it is accomplished through the entry of new firms; this is achieved as increased competition results in a lower price being charged in equilibrium, with a consequent reduction in 'deadweight' welfare loss.

5.3 CONCLUDING REMARKS

By permitting the consideration of a case where the introduction of new products leads to the complete displacement of existing ones, the preceding analysis suggests that in determining the effect of product innovation on the equilibrium level of employment, the primary factor involved is what we have called the 'welfare' effect. The interesting point, in looking at the employment-creating effect on product innovations in a general equilibrium setting, is the part played by the 'displacement' effect. In the 'Chamberlinian' setting considered in Chapter 4, there was a clear intuitive link between the 'displacement' effect and the 'welfare' effect. The introduction of goods which were close substitutes involved a large 'displacement' effect and a small 'welfare' effect, and so had little impact on employment. What the 'vertical' differentiation case underlines, is that even when the displacement effects are very large, the employment-creating effects of product innovation may be significant—all the more so when the introduction of new product *by new firms* enhances competition, and so further raises consumer welfare.

Thus, and in order to return briefly once again to my main theme, the present chapter reinforces the conclusions of Chapter 4 in that we have again shown that product innovation will have a favourable impact effect on the equilibrium level of employment, that is, even its short-run effect holding nominal aggregate expenditure constant will be positive. This is in contrast to the case of process innovation which, as noted in the general equilibrium framework of Chapter 3, and as suggested by the partial equilibrium analysis of Chapter 2, may well have a negative impact effect.

APPENDIX

In this appendix I will prove the proposition asserted in section 5.2 above, namely that provided the income distribution is of a specific range the elasticity of demand for u_2 will be sufficiently greater than unity to make $d\Pi_2/dp_2 < 0$ on the left of the kink associated with $\bar{p}_2$ (Figure 5.6) but less than unity to the right of this kink.

First consider the elasticity on the left of the kink associated with $\bar{p}_2$. From (15') and (13')

$$\eta = \frac{\left[\dfrac{de^*}{dp_2}\, u_2 \left(1 - \dfrac{p_2}{e^*}\right) + u_2 \log_e \left(\dfrac{b}{e^*}\right)\right]}{(u_2{:}b - e^*) - u_2 p_2 \log_e(b/e^*)}\, .$$

Hence,

$$\eta > 1 \text{ iff } \frac{de^*}{dp_2}\frac{p_2}{e^*}\left(1 - \frac{p_2}{e^*}\right) + 2 \frac{p_2}{e^*} \log_e \left(\frac{b}{e^*}\right) > \frac{b}{e^*} - 1. \text{(A)}$$

Since from (10) or (12), $de^*/dp_2 > 0$, (A) indicates that a sufficiently narrow distribution of income will guarantee that η is sufficiently greater than unity to make $d\Pi_2/dp_2 < 0$ for all p_2 up to $\bar{p}_2$.

Next consider the elasticity to the right of the kink associated with $\bar{p}_2$. To the right of $\bar{p}_2$, $de^*/dp_2 = 0$, and, as can also be seen from (14') and (16), in this case,

$$\eta = \frac{p_2 \log_e (b/a)}{(b - a) - p_2 \log_e (b/a)}\, . \tag{B}$$

Now, $\quad \eta < 1 \text{ iff } 2 \dfrac{p_2}{a} \log_e \left(\dfrac{b}{a}\right) < \dfrac{b}{a} - 1\, . \tag{C}$

With $p_2 < \bar{p}_2 = [(u_2 - u_0)/u_2]a$ it is sufficient for (C) to hold that $2[(u_2 - u_0)/u_2] \log_e (b/a) < (b/a) - 1$ given that, from (B), η is decreasing in p_2.

Clearly there is a range of values of a that make the distribution of income such that both (A) and (C) are satisfied.

NOTES

1. Main references are: Gabszewicz and Thisse (1980), and Shaked and Sutton (1983a,b). The model described here follows Gabszewicz (1981).

2. As already indicated, I am assuming that this is the unit variable cost for all quality goods.

3. The demand schedule of firm n, is $X_n = b - e_n$ where, from $(1')$ $e_n = [u_n/(u_n - u_{n-1})]p_n - [u_{n-1}/(u_n - u_{n-1})]p_{n-1}$, so that $X_n = b - [u_n/(u_n - u_{n-1})]p_n + [u_{n-1}/(u_n - u_{n-1})]p_{n-1}$.

4. It is as if workers were equally efficient (in output per hour), but differed in having various numbers of hours, e, available and we measured by ω the reservation hourly wage rate. Thus each worker decides on the basis of $(1')$ whether or not to supply a fixed number of hours, this being different for different workers.

5. This must be distinguished from the introduction of a new good in addition to u_2, as the possibility arises that the monopolist might 'segment the market' by offering both goods. This will not, however, be optimal if the range of incomes is sufficiently narrow, though the proof is by no means easy; *see* Gabszewicz *et al.* (1982).

6. Alternatively we can explain what happens in this case as follows. A worker of income e is indifferent between the outside good and one unit of u_2 with $e - p_2$ of the outside good when $p_2 = [(u_2 - u_0)/u_2]e$, and he is indifferent between the outside good and one unit of u_3 with $e - p_3$ of the outside good when $p_3 = [(u_3 - u_0)/u_3]e$. The difference between these, that is, $[(u_0/u_2) - (u_0/u_3)]e$ gives the willingness to pay by a worker of income e for the improvement in quality from u_2 to u_3. Clearly this willingness is increasing in income.

   The difference between the prices in the new equilibrium and the old equilibrium is $\bar{p}_3 - \bar{p}_2 = u_0[(1/u_2) - (1/u_3)]a$, that is, all workers with $e > a$ would be willing to pay more in equilibrium for the improvement in quality than they actually pay. There is, therefore, an increase in the utility score of all workers of $e > a$ and thus an increase in the value of ω that would make these workers stay unemployed, as depicted in Figure 5.10.

7. Notice that this is to the right of VL'_1 of Figure 5.8, defined by $(18')$.

8. Since $\bar{p}_3 = [(u_3 - u_0)/u_3]a$, since $\bar{p}_3 - p_3'' = (u_2/u_3)\{[(u_2 - u_0)/u_2]a - c\} = (u_2/u_3)(\bar{p}_2 - c) > 0$.

PART TWO:
The Effect of Innovation in the Long run

6 The Effect on Innovation in the Long Run under Price Flexibility

6.1 INTRODUCTION

In the present chapter, and in Chapter 7, I have two main aims, both related to limitations in the analyses of Part One. In Part One, I examined the short-run impact effect of innovation on employment holding aggregate nominal expenditure constant. My first aim in these two chapters is to endogenise aggregate expenditure. I do this in two contrasting ways: I use a simplified variation of a model first employed by Hicks in *Capital and Time* (1973) first under a flexprice (neoclassical) assumption (in the present chapter) and then under a fixprice (neo-Keynesian) assumption (in Chapter 7), to examine the transition path an economy would follow were a Walrasian equilibrium to be disturbed by a process innovation.

Whilst in the first case I get convergence to a new full employment Walrasian equilibrium, (assuming certain stability conditions are satisfied), whatever the short-run effect of the innovation on labour demand, in the second case, not only do I get an adverse short-run effect on labour demand (a result already examined in the context of a one-sector model in 2.4), but find that the long-run equilibrium may exhibit dynamic instability in the sense that the transition path does not converge to long-run equilibrium but involves ever increasing unemployment.

My second aim in this and the next chapter is, by going beyond the short run, to try to throw light on the conditions or mechanisms that may create adverse effects on labour demand and employment during the capital accumulation process induced by innovation. That is, I wish to study those aspects of technical change repercussions that arise in connection with the process of capital formation. To do so the model used will now include a capital good sector.

It will be helpful to try to make clear, at this point, how this latter aspect of the present investigations relates to the analyses of Part One. In section 2.2 I used a partial equilibrium model to obtain the conditions that, if present, would result in technical change reducing the marginal product of labour in the short run. It was Ricardo's argument, and this argument (as noted in the introduction) has been repeated by Hicks more recently, that were this to occur, even in the presence of real wage stickiness, there would be a reversal of the short-run increase in unemployment in the long run, as the capital accumulation process induced by the technical change increased the marginal product of labour. The present chapter produces a formal analysis of this claim by providing an analysis of what I shall term the Ricardo case. This involves obtaining answers to two important questions. In a two-sector economy, where one of the sectors produces a capital good, (a) what are the factors that lead to a reduction in labour demand in the short run? and (b) if the real wage were rigid, will the capital accumulation process induced by the technical change ensure that unemployment is eliminated in the long run?

Finally, the present chapter deals with another question: after process innovation will the induced capital accumulation process lead smoothly to a new Walrasian equilibrium? Or will the relevant economic variables overshoot their new Walrasian equilibrium values before eventually settling down at these values? I find that, in the present model, only when the effect of technical change is neutral as between the consumption and capital good sectors will the transition path to the new Walrasian equilibrium be a smooth one. In all other cases, the market-clearing real wage (the variable of main interest) will overshoot its new Walrasian equilibrium value before settling down at this value. This implies that even when the initial technological change raises the marginal product of labour everywhere, downward flexibility of the real wage is required along the transition path if the new Walrasian equilibrium is to be attained.[1]

6.2 A MODEL

In this section I will use a simplified variation of a model first employed by Hicks in *Capital and Time*. Hicks' preoccupations, unlike ours, were mainly growth theoretic. He, therefore, did not explore the issues to be discussed below. On the other hand, even though growth theory is not my concern, to describe the long-run effects of embodied technical change it is necessary to deal with investment, that is, a capital accumulation process.

I will assume that a consumption and a capital good are produced, their respective outputs being X and K (subscripts will be used to denote time periods). The consumer good is non-storable (lasting for one period). Capital is measured by its capacity to produce consumption output; the capital-good machine being considered as a capacity unit, a piece of equipment that has the capacity to produce a fixed arbitrary quantity of the consumption good per period (this quantity being the measurement unit for consumption output).

A machine is produced by using a_k units of labour with a lag of one period. It lasts for one period, during which time it may be used in conjunction with a_c units of labour to produce one unit of the consumer good. In other words, the investment of wa_k units of the consumer good in period t, results in a capacity unit in $t + 1$. Labour supply is assumed to be fixed at L units. The amount of labour used to construct machines will be denoted by L^k and that used to utilise them by L^c. Of course

$$L^k = a_k K \quad \text{and} \quad L^c = a_c X \tag{1}$$

Finally, I will assume that (a) all wages are consumed and (b) the opportunity cost of capital is zero; this implies that all realised profits—assumed to be the only source of finance—

are automatically invested in the construction of new machines.

The Walrasian Stationary Equilibrium

In a stationary state, a fixed number of machines will be produced and utilised every period. Full employment requires that employment constructing and utilising these machines is equal to labour supply—that is, if $X = K$ is the number of machines,

$$X(a_k + a_c) = L \Rightarrow X = L/(a_c + a_k) \ . \tag{2}$$

Further, in equilibrium, firms will not desire to expand or contract their capacity; with a zero interest rate, this requires that $p - wa_c = wa_k$ which requires that

$$w/p = 1/(a_c + a_k) \ ; \tag{3}$$

(2) and (3) give the stationary Walrasian equilibrium values of consumption (and machine) output and real wage respectively. From (1), in this equilibrium,

$$L^k/a_k = L^c/a_c = L/(a_c + a_k) \ . \tag{4}$$

Consider now a technical change that leads to a change of a_c and a_k to a_c' and a_k', (using primes to denote 'new' values). The new Walrasian equilibrium will be defined by:

$$X' = L/(a_c' + a_k') \tag{2'}$$

$$(w/p)' = 1/(a_c' + a_k') \tag{3'}$$

and

$$L^{k'}/a_k' = L^{c'}/a_c' = L/(a_c' + a_k') \ . \tag{4'}$$

Also, from equations (4) and (4'),

$$\frac{L^{k'}}{L^k} = \frac{(a_c/a_k) + 1}{(a_c'/a_k') + 1} \quad \text{and} \quad \frac{L^{c'}}{L^c} = \frac{(a_k/a_c) + 1}{(a_k'/a_c') + 1} \ . \tag{5}$$

It will be convenient to use the symbols h and H to denote $h = a_k/a_k'$ and $H = a_c/a_c'$. Neutral technical change is defined as the case where $h = H$. In this case $a_c/a_k = a_c'/a_k' \Rightarrow L^{k'} = L^k$ and $L^{c'} = L^c$, that is, the ratio of constructional to utilisational labour remains unchanged. Technical change is biased if $h \neq H$. If $h < H \Rightarrow L^{k'} > L^k$ and $L^{c'} < L^c$; if $h > H \Rightarrow L^{k'} < L^k$ and $L^{c'} > L^c$.

6.3 THE TRANSITION PATH UNDER PRICE FLEXIBILITY

Here I describe the transition path to the new Walrasian equilibrium following the technical change. First I look at period 1 and then I generalise. In period 1 all existing machines are old ones—a number L_0^k/a_k of them—and hence $L_1^c = (a_c/a_k) L_0^k$. Labour available to construct machines is therefore $L_1^k = L - L_1^c = L - L_0^c = L_0^k$, that is, the same as in period 0. Profits, π, at period 0 real wages, will be

$$\pi_1 = \left[1 - \left(\frac{w}{p}\right)_0 a_c\right] \frac{L_0^k}{a_k} = \left[1 - \frac{a_c}{a_c + a_k}\right] \frac{L_0^k}{a_k} = \left(\frac{w}{p}\right)_0 L_0^k \; ;$$

(using (3)), that is, with $(w/p)0 = (w/p)_1$,

labour demand $= [\pi_1/(w/p)_0] + L_1^c = L_0^k + L_0^c = L =$ labour supply,

and hence $(w/p)_0$ is the equilibrium real wage in period 1 with number of machines constructed being $K_1 = L_1^k/a_k' = X_2$.

Given that $L_1^k = L_0^k$, I can now describe the transition path of the market-clearing real wage and of machine construction. (Since $X_t = L_{t-1}^k/a_k'$, the transition path of capacity, and hence of consumption output, follows.) For $t \geqslant 2$ all machines are new machines, so for $t \geqslant 2$ $\pi_t = [1 - (w/p)_t a_c']$ (L_{t-1}^k/a_k') and demand for labour to construct machines is $\pi_t/(w/p)_t$, so that total demand for labour $= \pi_t/(w/p)_t + a_c'(L_{t-1}^k/a_k') = L_{t-1}^k/a_k'(w/p)_t$. Hence, labour market equilibrium requires that the real wage rate is

$$\left(\frac{w}{p}\right)_t = \frac{L_{t-1}^k}{a_k' L} \; . \tag{6}$$

Further, the amount of labour available to construct machines is, for $t \geq 2$,

$$L_t^k = L - L_t^c = L - a_c' \, (L_{t-1}^k/a_k') \ . \tag{7}$$

It may easily be shown that the value of L^k tends to

$$L_0^k\left[1 + \left(\frac{a_c}{a_k} - \frac{a_c'}{a_k'}\right)' - \frac{a_c'}{a_k'}\left(\frac{a_c}{a_k} - \frac{a_c'}{a_k'}\right) + \left(\frac{a_c'}{a_k'}\right)^2\left(\frac{a_c}{a_k} - \frac{a_c'}{a_k'}\right)\dots\right] \tag{8}$$

where L_0^k is its value in period 1, whilst the value of the real wage rate tends to

$$\frac{L^k}{La_k'}\left[1 + \left(\frac{a_c}{a_k} - \frac{a_c'}{a_k'}\right) - \frac{a_c'}{a_k'}\left(\frac{a_c}{a_k} - \frac{a_c'}{a_k'}\right) + \left(\frac{a_c'}{a_k'}\right)^2\left(\frac{a_c}{a_k} - \frac{a_c'}{a_k'}\right)\dots\right] \tag{9}$$

where $\dfrac{L^k}{La_k'}$ is the value of the real wage rate in period 2.

That is, the value of L^k tends to $a_k'L/(a_c' + a_k')$ and the value of the real wage to $1/(a_c' + a_k')$, that is, to their new Walrasian equilibrium values, *provided* $a_c' < a_k'$. The latter is the usual stability condition; in more conventional models it appears in the form of a requirement that capital intensity in machine production is less than it is in the production of the consumption good (*see*, for example, Morishima's *Theory of Economic Growth*, p. 21). We will assume that this condition is satisfied (for an attempt to justify this *see* Hicks' *Capital and Time*, p. 105).

Now, expressions (8) and (9) may also be written as follows:

$$L_0^k\left[1 + \frac{a_c'}{a_k'}\left(\frac{H}{h} - 1\right)\left(1 - \frac{a_c'}{a_k'} + \dots\right)\right] \tag{8'}$$

and

$$\frac{L^k}{La'_k}\left[1 + \frac{a'_c}{a'_k}\left(\frac{H}{h} - 1\right)\left(1 - \frac{a'_c}{a'_k} + \ldots\right)\right] \tag{9'}$$

These expressions enable one to examine the behaviour of the real wage and machine construction during the Traverse under different assumptions concerning the bias of the technical change. I will distinguish between three cases: (i) $H = h$, the neutral technical change case, (ii) $h \neq H$, h, $H >$ 1, where technical change is biased, but not strongly, and finally, (iii) $h < 1$ (H must then be greater than 1 for the innovation to be adopted): this I term, following Hicks, the *Ricardo case*; in this case there is actually an *increase* in the amount of labour required to produce machines, the innovation being 'strongly capital-using'. I will consider each of these in turn:[2]

Case i: $H = h$
It is clear from (8') and (9') that there is, in this case, a smooth convergence to the new Walrasian equilibrium—from (8'), L^k attains its new Walrasian equilibrium value in period 1 (this is equal to L_0^k, that is, the old equilibrium value, as can be seen from (5)). From (9'), the real wage rate attains its new equilibrium value in period 2, being, in period 1, equal to $(w/p)_0$ (when $h = H \Rightarrow a_c/a_k = a'_c/a'_k \Rightarrow L^k/La'_k = 1/(a'_c + a'_k) =$ new Walrasian equilibrium value of the real wage).

Case ii: $(H \neq h); H, h > 1$
If $H > h$, that is, the main saving occurs in machine utilisation, machine construction L^k/a'_k and the real wage overshoot their new equilibrium values in period 2 and period 3 respectively, and then oscillate around these values in a converging manner. If $H < h$, that is, the main saving is in machine construction, L^k/a'_k and the real wage overshoot their new equilibrium values in periods 1 and 2, respectively, and then oscillate around these values in a converging manner. These two cases (together with the neutral and the Ricardo cases) are depicted in Figure 6.1 (which shows the transition path of machine construction), and Figure 6.2 (which shows the transition path of the real wage). It will

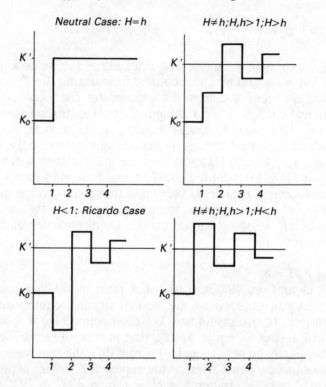

Figure 6.1:   *Transition paths of machine construction under diffe-rent assumptions concerning bias*

$K_0 = X_0$ = capacity and output at old equilibrium ($=L^k/a_k$); $K' = X'$ = capacity and output at new equilibrium ($=L^{k'}/a'_k$); $H = a_c/a'_c$; $h = a_k/a'_k$; it is assumed that $a'_c < a'_k$, that is, the stability condition is satisfied.

help to interpret these two figures more clearly if we rewrite equations (8′) and (9′) so that we obtain the *deviation* of machine construction and the real wage from their new equilibrium values, $L^{k'}/a'_k$ and $(w/p)'$, respectively. First note that from (5)

$$L_0^k = L^k = L^{k'} \cdot z \qquad (10)$$

and from (3′) and (4′)

$$L^k/La'_k = (L^{k'}/La'_k) \cdot z = (w/p)' \cdot z \qquad (11)$$

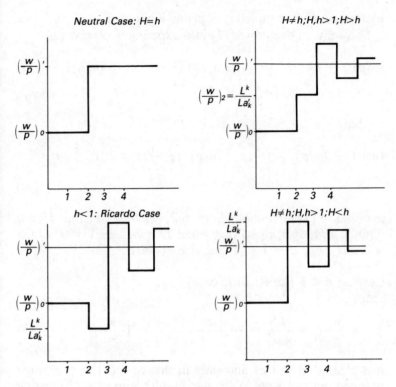

Figure 6.2: *Transition paths of the market clearing real wage under different assumptions concerning bias*

$(w/p)_0$ = real wage at old equilibrium; $(w/p)'$ = real wage at new equilibrium; $(w/p)_2 = L_k/La'_k$; $H = a_c/a'_c$; $h = a_k/a'_k$; it is assumed that $a'_c < a'_k$, that is, that the stability condition is satisfied.

where

$$z = 1 + \frac{(a'_c/a'_k) - (a_c/a_k)}{(a_c/a_k) + 1} . \tag{12}$$

Substituting first into expression (8) equation (10) and dividing by a'_k gives

$$\left(\frac{L^{k'}}{a'_k}\right) z + \left(\frac{L^{k'}}{a'_k}\right) z \left(\frac{a_c}{a_k} - \frac{a'_c}{a'_k}\right) \left[1 - \frac{a'_c}{a'_k} + \left(\frac{a'_c}{a'_k}\right)^2 - \ldots\right] \tag{8''}$$

from which it may be seen that

$$L^{k'}/a'_k - L^k_t/a'_k = (-1)^t (L^{k'}/a'_k)(z-1)(a'_c/a'_k)^{t-1}; \quad t \geq 1 ; \tag{13}$$

114   *Effect of Innovation in the Long Run*

expression (13) completely explains Figure 6.1.
  Secondly, substituting (11) into expression (9) gives

$$(w/p)'z + (w/p)'z \, (a_c/a_k - a_c'/a_k') \, [1 - a_c'/a_k' + (a_c'/a_k')^2 - ...]$$

$$(9'')$$

so that

$$(w/p)' - (w/p)_t = (-1)^{t-1} \, (w/p)' \, (z - 1) \, (a_c'/a_k')^{t-2}; \quad t \geq 2;$$

$$(14)$$

expression (14) explains Figure 6.2. (Remember that $H \gtreqless h$
implies $a_c/a_k \gtreqless a_c'/a_k'$ so that when $H = h$, $z - 1 = 0$, whilst
when $H > h$, $z - 1 < 0$ and vice versa.)

Case iii: $h < 1$ The Ricardo case)
Since

$$\left(\frac{w}{p}\right)_2 = \frac{L^k}{La_k'} = \frac{a_k}{a_k'(a_c + a_k)} = h \cdot \left(\frac{w}{p}\right)_0 \qquad (15)$$

it is clear that in this and only in this case is the real wage
reduced below its *old* Walrasian equilibrium value following
technical change, that is, *only when $h < 1$ is labour demand
reduced, in comparison to demand at old equilibrium, following the introduction of the innovation.*
  As can be seen from (8), machine construction (L_0^k/a_k') in
period 1 (and hence, capacity in period 2) is below its old
Walrasian equilibrium value. This is, of course, due to the
increase in the amount of labour required to construct
machines. The reduction in capacity means that profits in
period 2, at the old Walrasian equilibrium level of the real
wage, are not sufficient, when invested, to absorb all labour:
labour demand in period 2 is $[\pi_2/(w/p)_2] + L_2^c = [\pi_2/(w/p)_2] +
a_c'(L_0^k/a_k') = L_0^k/[a_k'(w/p)_2]$ which, if $(w/p)_2 = (w/p)_0$, is less
than $L = L_0^k/[a_k(w/p)_0]$ if the real wage is reduced.
  Nevertheless, as can be seen from Figure 6.2, the reduction is temporary: machine construction and the real wage
are above their new equilibrium values in periods 2 and 3
respectively. Furthermore, even if the real wage were fixed,

the reduction in labour demand (and unemployment)—
being the result of a 'capital shortage'—will be eliminated by
the process of capital accumulation that follows. For even if
the real wage remained at the old equilibrium level in period
2, machine construction in this period would be greater than
in period 1 since profit would be increased in this period
(relative to period 1), due to the reduction in a_c^3. So, capacity
will increase in period 3 relative to period 2, and so on.
Basically, with the real wage below its *new* Walrasian
equilibrium value, firms will be increasing capacity and
labour demand until unemployment is eliminated and excess
labour demand appears. This explains Ricardo's conten-
tion—he was assuming a subsistence real wage to start
with—that technical change *may* reduce labour demand and
create unemployment, but that this will be only temporary,
capital accumulation leading eventually to a reversal of this
situation.

The preceding analysis may be seen as an explicit restate-
ment of the argument offered by Ricardo.[4]

APPENDIX

This appendix reviews Chapter 12 of Stoneman (1983),
which deals with issues related to our own concerns in
Chapters 6 and 7. Stoneman provides an alternative two-
sector model for the examination of the long-run effect of
technical change on output and employment (section 12.3
and appendix to Chapter 12). In this model (as in the present
one, but unlike the one employed in Chapter 7) it is assumed
that 'all wages are consumed and all profits are saved and
invested' (*ibid.* p. 178), this, according to the author, being
the most fundamental weakness of the model (*ibid.* p. 179).
This is especially so, in view of the fact that 'wages are
assumed to be determined independently of the demand for
labour' (*ibid.* p. 178), since in disequilibrium firms' investment plans are likely to be affected by perceptions of
possibly facing constraints in consumption good markets—
the implications of incorporating this into the analysis are
explored in Chapter 7 below, where a quantity constraint

model is used. On the other hand, Stoneman's model has the advantage of incorporating specific diffusion profiles of the new technology to reflect the fact 'that new technologies take time to spread' (*ibid.* p. 178). The speed of diffusion is found to be an important determinant of the impact of the new technology during the transition phase.

In Chapter 12 Stoneman also discusses the neoclassical (aggregate production function), neo-Austrian and input–output approaches to the *empirical testing* of the impact of technical change on output and employment (section 12.4, pp. 181–94). Especially useful is his summary of his earlier work (Stoneman, 1976) in which he uses 'an essentially Austrian representation of technology combined with an actual diffusion path of computer usage and generates a series of job losses and gains resulting from computer use in the UK' (*ibid.* p. 189). This study provides an illustration of how, according to the author,

an analysis of the transition path can yield results so different from comparative statics analysis. Even though computerisation could lead to labour saving comparing computerised with non-computerised economies, this does not mean that those labour savings will be realised immediately, or that during the transition stage that there will be a net reduction in labour demand (*ibid.* p. 191).

On the other hand, the author concludes, the exercise is open to the basic criticism that 'The output of the economy is assumed to be independent of the use of the new technology, and this is probably unrealistic' (*ibid.* p. 191).

Whilst input–output models may also be in general criticised for failing to take account of the demand impact of the new technology, an example 'of the importance of the inclusion of this in such models' is provided by Wilson and Whitley's (1982) use of 'an augmented input–output model to look at the possible effects of microelectronics' (Stoneman, *ibid.* p. 192). In Wilson and Whitley's simulation exercise the direct labour-displacing effects of the technical change induced increases in output per man

are offset partly by increases in demand through resulting cost and price reduction. These offsetting effects are calculated at the aggregate level to approximate 50 per cent of any initial direct reduction in employment. In addition to these first-round compensation effects, the authors argue that further increases in demand and thus employment and output will come from 'second-round' compensation because of

1. extra investment demand for installing new technology,
2. changes in intermediate demands,
3. improved trade performance from improved non-price competitiveness.

The sum of these three effects, they calculate, will more than offset the gap between first-round indirect effects and the direct effect (*ibid.* p. 192–194).

Whilst, as Stoneman notes, 'in generating second-round compensation effects the assumptions are somewhat arbitrary', it is true that 'as a simulation exercise the whole process is illuminating' (*ibid.* p. 194). Furthermore, 'the calculation that about 50 per cent of direct displacement can be offset by first-round compensation has been found in other applications of input–output models to these types of questions; see Stoneman *et al.* (1982)' (*ibid.* p. 194).

NOTES

1. For an alternative two-sector model *see* Stoneman (1983) section 12.3 and appendix to Chapter 12. In the appendix to the present chapter I review Stoneman's discussion.
2. The case $H < 1$ does not involve anything of significance that is not covered in the $H \neq h$ case.
3. Profit in period 2 is $\pi_2 = [1 - (w/p)_0 \, a'_c] \, (L_0^k/a_k)$, whilst in period 1 it is $\pi_1 = [1 - (w/p)_0 \, a_c] \cdot L_0^k/a_k$, L_0^k/a'_k being machine construction in period 1 and hence capacity in period 2. L_0^k/a_k is the old equilibrium capacity. But $[1 - (w/p)_0 \, a'_c] \, [(w/p)_0 \, a'_k]$ is the rate or profit *at the old equilibrium* real wage *after* the innovation, whilst $[1 - (w/p)_0 \, a_c] \, [(w/p)_0 \, a_k]$ is the old equilibrium rate of profit. The former must be greater for the innovation to be introduced, hence $\pi_2 > \pi_1$.
4. *See also* section 7.3 and section 8.3 for discussion related to this.

7 The Effect of Innovation in the Long Run under Quantity Constraints

7.1 INTRODUCTION

As already indicated (section 6.1 above) in this chapter the long-run effects of technical change are considered under the assumption that w and p are fixed in the short run, a temporary equilibrium being achieved in each period by quantity rationing. Thus, with the previous chapter, the present chapter completes my discussion of the long-run effect of innovation under alternative assumptions concerning price flexibility.

A brief description of the structure of the fixprice temporary equilibrium models is useful at this point:

At the outset of any given period, prices are quoted, e.g. by the sellers, in the light of their past experience and their expectations of the state of the economy in the coming and future periods. Once these prices are quoted, they cannot be changed until the next period. At these prices, the demands and supplies currently expressed *ex ante* by the agents may not be compatible. In that case, it is postulated that there is an allocation mechanism (or a rationing scheme) which makes the agents' realised (or *ex post*) transactions sum to zero. Then the economy moves to the next date and new prices may be quoted. The rules obeyed by an allocation mechanism are simple. If at the ruling prices, the demand and supply currently expressed by the agents on a given market are compatible, then all agents should realise their plans. If there is an excess demand, then all sellers should realise their plans, while some buyers must be rationed.[1]

118

In discussions on how disequilibrium affects behaviour emphasis is placed on the so-called 'spillover effects': 'When one market fails to clear, rational economic agents may revise the demands and supplies that they present to other markets'; these revised demands and supplies being Clower's 'effective' demands and supplies—as opposed to the originally expressed 'notional' ones. This means that, in contrast to equilibrium models, in which only relative prices affect behaviour, under disequilibrium the level of transactions in the market that fails to clear will enter the revised demands and supplies expressed in other markets. Applied to firm behaviour, recognising disequilibrium situations implies the recognition of the need by the firm to forecast

both the current and the future demand for output; the first in order to determine how much current output to produce, and the second to determine how much investment to undertake in order to produce future output. In a world with complete, continually equilibriated future markets the investment decision depends only on a vector of future prices. In a world with no future markets, firms must guess at the level of future demand. A good indicator of this future demand is presumably current demand; hence investment decisions will depend on firm's expectations about current demand.[2]

This argument is incorporated below (section 7.2) in the Hicks-type model set-up in Chapter 6; I use this revised model to study the sequence of temporary equilibria generated by embodied technical change when prices are fixed in the short run. The particular form that this argument takes, in terms of my model, is that firms' desired machine construction during period t is equal to the consumption demand they expect for that period (the latter indicating their forecast of future consumption demand). Different assumptions will be made concerning the calculation of expected current demand. First, in section 7.2 I assume that firms base their investment on an expectation of current demand that is equal to the output they sold in the period before the current one. That is, firms are assumed to have a certain expectation of current demand that is equal to last period's output and to construct a number of machines equal to that. In the first appendix to this chapter I present an extension of this, derived by allowing the sales constraint to be uncertain (in a manner recently examined by Malinvaud, 1980); this allows profitability to affect current investment demand. Finally, in Appendix 2 of this chapter I look briefly at the implications for the issues under discussion here of firms perceiving kinks on their demand curves. This may be the result of imperfect information on the part of consumers, as noted recently by Negishi (1979). Kinked demand curves have also been shown to arise in (partial equilibrium) models of spatial competition when the existence of an outside good is assumed (Salop, 1979).[3]

7.2 THE INSTABILITY OF THE TRANSITION PATH UNDER QUANTITY CONSTRAINTS

In this section I reintroduce the model developed in Chapter 6 to examine the sequence of temporary equilibria (with p and w fixed in the short run) generated by embodied technical change. We must now distinguish between 'effective' and 'notional' demands and supplies and 'realised' quantities. Superscripts 'd', 's' and 'e' will denote 'demand', 'supply' and 'employment' respectively. When the superscript 'd' or 's' is primed it denotes an effective (otherwise a notional) quantity.

The three main assumptions to be used in this section are:

A1. The 'myopic investment rule':

$$K_t^d = X_t^{d,ex} = X_{t-1} \tag{1}$$

where K_t^d is demand for machines to be constructed in t, $X_t^{d,ex}$ is expected consumption demand for period t, and X_{t-1} is output (sales) in period $t-1$.

A2. Technical change affects the labour coefficients so that $a_c' \leq a_c$ and $a_k' \leq a_k$. No more specific assumption is required concerning the bias of innovation.

A3. The wage bargain is made in real terms, the real wage adjusting each period according to the following rule:

$$(w/p)_t = (w/p)_{t-1} + \epsilon(L^{d'}_{t-1} - L) , \qquad (2)$$

ϵ being a positive constant. (No distinction need be made, for the cases to be considered below, between the *notional* labour supply, L, and *effective* supply— that is, labour supply when consumers are constrained in the consumer good market; this point is proved later in this section.)

Output and employment are given by

$$X_t = \min(X^{d'}_t , X^s_t) \qquad (3)$$

and $\qquad L^e_t = \min (L^{d'}_t , L) \qquad (4)$

where $\qquad X^s_t = K_{t-1} \qquad (5)$

is productive capacity (or, notional supply of consumption) in t; (strictly speaking, output is the minimum of effective demand and *effective* supply of the consumer good, but in the following firms will never be constrained by labour in utilising fully their capacity). Following our previous practice of denoting by superscripts 'k' and 'c' the construction and consumer sectors respectively, we may now write:

$$L^{d'}_t = L^{k,d'}_t + L^{c,d'}_t \qquad (6)$$

and $\qquad X^{d'}_t = (w/p)_t (L^{k,e}_t + L^{c,e}_t) \qquad (7)$

whilst $\qquad X^d_t = (w/p)_t L. \qquad (8)$

We must then write expressions for *effective* demands for labour for construction and machine utilisation. First, since the firm's demand for machines is not, by A1., affected by what is currently happening in other markets,

$$L^{k,d'}_t = L^{k,d}_t = a_k K^d_t . \qquad (9)$$

On the other hand, firms will demand an amount of labour for machine utilisation equal to their notional demand, $a_c X^s_t$, only if X^s_t can be fully utilised. If firms can sell only an output

$X_t < X_t^s$, then their effective demand for utilisation labour will be

$$L_t^{c,d'} = a_c X_t \ . \tag{10}$$

Finally, (realised) employment for construction and machine utilisation will be,

$$L_t^{k,e} = \min (L_t^{k,d'} \ , \ L_t^k) \quad \text{and} \quad L_t^{c,e} = \min (L_t^{c,d'} \ , \ L_t^c) \tag{11}$$

where L_t^k , L_t^c stand for labour supply to construction and utilisation, respectively. How are we to interpret these quantities? As we have seen (section 6.2) in Walrasian equilibrium, the division of labour is determined by the technical coefficients ($L^k/L^c = a_k/a_c$). The least ambiguous way of interpreting the labour supply variables in equations (11), is to assume that they are equal to the original Walrasian equilibrium values of L^k and L^c (the time subscript is then dropped), and this is what I am going to do. Note that this is an inessential assumption in the sense that, as will be shown below, no change in the original Walrasian equilibrium values of labour supply to construction and machine utilisation is required during the Traverse following the technical change.[4] So, (11) may be written as

$$L_t^{k,e} = \min (L_t^{k,d'} \ , \ L^k) \quad \text{and} \quad L_t^{c,e} = \min (L_t^{c,d'} \ , \ L^c) \tag{11'}$$

where L^k and L^c are the supply (and employment) of labour in construction and utilisation, respectively, in the original Walrasian equilibrium (these values are given by equations (4) of Section 6.2).

I start from a full employment Walrasian equilibrium defined by (see also 6.2),

$$X_0^s = X_0 = K_0 = L/(a_c + a_k) \quad \text{and} \quad (w/p)_0 = 1/(a_c + a_k) \ .$$
$$\tag{12}$$

The new Walrasian equilibrium is:

$$X^s = X = K = L/(a'_c + a'_k) \quad \text{and} \quad (w/p) = 1/(a'_c + a'_k) .$$

$$(12')$$

Consider period 1, the period the innovation is introduced. From (12) and (5), $X_1^s = X_0$; from (2), $(w/p)_1 = (w/p)_0$; from A.1, (9), $(11')$ and $a'_k < a_k$, $K_1^d = X_0 \Rightarrow L_1^{k,d'} = a'_k X_0 < L^k \Rightarrow L_{1,}^{k\,e} = L_1^{k,d'}$ and $K_1 = K_1^d$.

The decline in constructional employment implies a decline in effective demand for consumption since $(w/p)_1 (L_1^{k,e} + a_c X_1^s) < X_1^s = X_0 = (w/p)_1 L = (w/p)_1 (L^k + a_c X_1^s)$ and, therefore, firms will employ an amount of labour to utilise capacity, $L_1^{c,d'} < a_c X_1^s = L^c \Rightarrow L_1^{c,e} = L_1^{c,d'} = a_c X_1$ (from (10)). Hence, $L_1^{d'} = L_1^{k,d'} + L_1^{c,d'} < L \Rightarrow L_1^e = L_1^{d'}$ (from (4)). Further, since from (7), $X_1^{d'} = (w/p)_1 (L_1^{k,e} + L_1^{c,e}) < X_1^s = (w/p)_1 L \Rightarrow X_1 = X_1^{d'}$ from equation (3). To summarize, in period 1, consumption output and employment for machine utilisation and construction will be given respectively by

$$X_1 = (w/p)_1 (L_1^{k,e} + L_1^{c,e}), \quad L_1^{c,e} = a_c X_1 \quad \text{and} \quad L_1^{k,e} = a'_k X_0.$$

Solving we obtain:

$$X_1 = (1/r_1)X_0 = (1/r_1)X_1^s$$

where $r_1 = [1 - (w/p)_1 a_c]/[(w/p)_1 a'_k] > 1$

(since $(w/p)_1 = (w/p)_0 = 1/(a_c + a_k)$ and $a'_k < a_k$); hence $X_1 < X_0$. Hence, in period 1, machine construction remains at the old equilibrium level whilst consumption output and employment decline, excess supply of labour leading to a decline in the real wage rate in period 2 according to equation (2).

Given the reduction in output and employment in period 1, I now show that this will continue indefinitely, under the present assumptions, the economy getting further and further away from the new Walrasian equilibrium with time. To show this consider a period $t + 1$, $t \geq 1$, and *assume* that

(i) $X_t < X_t^s \leq X_{t-1} = K_t$

(ii) $L_t^{k,e} = a_k' K_t < L_{t-1}^{k,e} \leqslant L^k$

(iii) $L_t^{c,e} = a_c' X_t < L_{t-1}^{c,e} \leqslant L^c$

(iv) $(w/p)_{t+1} < (w/p)_t \leqslant (w/p)_{t-1}$; $r_t > 1$.

Now, from (5), A1., and assumption (ii) above, $X_{t+1}^s = K_t = X_{t-1}$ (since $K_t = \min [K_t^d, (L^k/a_k')]$ and, from assumption (ii) $a_k' K_t < L^k, K_t = K_t^d$). From this, A1., and assumptions (i) and (ii): $K_{t+1}^d = X_t \Rightarrow L_{t+1}^{k,d'} = a_k' K_{t+1}^d = a'_k X_t < a_k' X_{t-1} = a_k' K_t = L_t^{k,e} < L^k$. Hence, from (11'), $L_{t+1}^{k,e} = L_{t+1}^{k,d'}$ and $K_{t+1} = K_{t+1}^d = X_t$. This implies that, taking into account assumption (iv) above,

$$(w/p)_{t+1} (L_{t+1}^{k,e} + a_c' X_{t+1}^s) < (w/p)_{t-1} (L_t^{k,e} + a_c' X_{t-1})$$

$$= X_{t-1} = X_{t+1}^s.$$

Hence, since from assumption (iii) above, $L_{t-1}^{c,e} \leqslant L^c$ firms will employ an amount of labour to utilise capacity, $L_{t+1}^{c,d'} < a'_c X_{t+1}^s = L_{t-1}^{c,e} \Rightarrow L_{t+1}^{c,e} = L_{t+1}^{c,d'} = a'_c X_{t+1}$ (from (11') and (10)). Therefore, taking account of (7), $X_{t+1}^{d'} = (w/p)_{t+1} (L_{t+1}^{k,e} + L_{t+1}^{c,e}) < X_{t+1}^s \Rightarrow X_{t+1} = X_{t+1}^{d'}$, from (3), and since $X_{t+1}^s = X_{t-1} = (w/p)_{t-1} (L_{t-1}^{c,e} + L_{t-1}^{k,e})$.

So, $X_{t+1} = (w/p)_{t+1} (L_{t+1}^{k,e} + L_{t+1}^{c,e})$,

$L_{t+1}^{c,e} = a_c' X_{t+1}$ and $L_{t+1}^{k,e} = a_k' X_t$

Solving we obtain:

$$X_{t+1} = (1/r_{t+1})X_t < X_t$$

Since

$$r_{t+1} =$$

$$[1 - (w/p)_{t+1} a_c']/[(w/p)_{t+1} a_k'] > r_t \text{ (since } (w/p)_{t+1} < (w/p)_t)$$

and $r_t > 1$, by assumption. Therefore $L_{t+1}^{c,e} < L_t^{c,e}$ and, as we have seen, $L_{t+1}^{k,e} < L_t^{k,e}$. Hence, $L_{t+1}^{d'} = L_{t+1}^e < L$, so that $(w/p)_{t+2} < (w/p)_{t+1}$.

So, having made assumptions (i)–(iv), I have shown that there is, in period $t + 1$, a reduction in consumption output and constructional and utilisational employment, as compared to period t; that $r_{t+1} > r_t$, and that there is a decrease in the real wage in $t + 2$ as compared to $t + 1$. Since assumptions (i)–(iv) have been shown to be true for $t = 1$, I have now also shown that in period 2 output and employment decrease further, $r_2 > r_1$, and $(w/p)_2 < (w/p)_1$. But this is sufficient to prove likewise that there is a further reduction in output and employment in period 3, that $r_3 > r_2$, and that $(w/p)_3 < (w/p)_2$, and so on.

Before I conclude I must return and try to justify one of the earlier assumptions. I said that no distinction need be made between notional and effective labour supply, implicitly assuming that consumers would not be constrained in the consumption good market, or, that notional consumption demand would be less than notional supply (that is, capacity) after the technical change. Only if this is valid will the above hold, for only then is it valid to argue that labour supply remains at its notional level. Now, in period 1, notional consumption demand $(w/p)_1 L$, is equal to capacity X_0; whilst in period 2, notional consumption demand $= (w/p)_2 L < X_0 = K_1 =$ capacity (since $(w/p)_2 < (w/p)_1$). But after period 2, whilst notional consumption demand is falling, as the real wage is being reduced, so does capacity (e.g., in period 3, capacity $= K_2 = X_1 < X_0$, etc.). Will the fall in capacity catch up with the fall in notional demand?[5] Consider period $t \geq 3$, and assume that in all periods between the original Walrasian equilibrium and t a temporary Keynesian equilibrium is established, with output and employment being progressively reduced. Now, notional demand in period t is $(w/p)_t L = (w/p)_{t-1} L + \epsilon(L_{t-1}^{d'} - L)L$ (from A.3). Hence,

$$(w/p)_t L = (w/p)_{t-1} L_{t-1}^e + (w/p)_{t-1}(L - L_{t-1}^e) + \epsilon L(L_{t-1}^e - L)^6$$

$$= X_{t-1} + (L - L_{t-1}^e)((w/p)_{t-1} - \epsilon L).$$

On the other hand, capacity in t is $X_t^s = K_{t-1} = X_{t-2}$ and $X_{t-2} > X_{t-1}$; thus since $(w/p)_{t-1} < (w/p) = 1/(a_c + a_k)$, for as long as ϵ is sufficiently high (as I will now assume), notional consumption demand remains below capacity (that is, below notional supply).

What I have shown in this section is that when firms are pessimistic about future demand, in the sense that they do not expect to be able to sell more than they have done in the past, embodied technical change leads to (or, one may say is equivalent to an exogenous) reduction in investment demand. This in turn reduces effective demand and leads to excess capacity. The latter seems to justify the initial pessimism and thus leads to further reductions in investment; this to further reductions in demand and increased excess capacity, and so on. This vicious circle could only be broken by an exogenous increase in demand as may be instituted by a 'pump-priming' government policy. Unless this occurs, the dynamic evolution of the real wage, output, and capacity utilisation will be as shown in the following figures. Figure 7.1 and 7.2 below depict the real wage and consumption output dynamics, respectively. Figure 7.3 illustrates the evolution of capacity utilisation. (Assuming uncertain sales constraints, as I do in Appendix 1 to this chapter, will not affect the substance of the present results.)

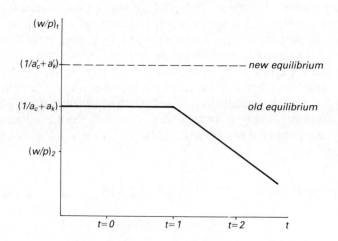

Figure 7.1   *Real wage dynamics*

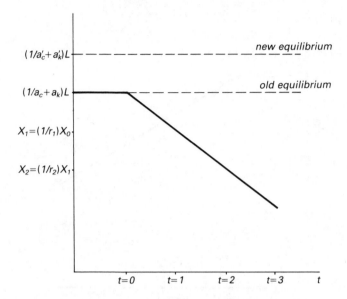

Figure 7.2   *Dynamics of consumption output*

Figure 7.3 depicts the evolution of the ratio X_t/X_t^s, that is, of the proportion of capacity utilised in period t. From period $t = 0$ to $t = 2$, capacity $X_0^s = X_1^s = X_2^s = X_0$; hence, (as is clear from p. 161 above),

$$X_0/X_0^s = 1 > X_1/X_1^s = X_1/X_0 = 1/r_1 > X_2/X_2^s = X_2/X_0 = 1/r_1r_2.$$

Capacity utilisation will continue declining after $t = 2$, since, as was shown, r is increasing. Thus, in period t, $t \geqslant 3$,

$$\frac{X_t}{X_t^s} = \frac{X_t X_{t-1}}{X_{t-1} X_{t-2}} = \frac{X_{t-1}}{r_t X_{t-2}} = \frac{1}{r_t r_{t-1}} < \frac{X_{t-1}}{X_{t-1}^s} = \frac{1}{r_{t-1} r_{t-2}} .$$

7.3   CONCLUDING REMARKS

What is important in obtaining the results of the present chapter, is not just the assumption of price and wage inflexibility, or the unrealistic assumption I made concerning

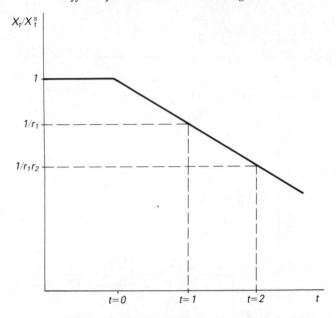

Figure 7.3   *Dynamics of capacity utilisation*

demand expectations (and this will be further clarified by the analysis of Appendix 1 to this chapter). It is also the further assumption that agents' optimising plans are influenced by price and wage inflexibility. Most importantly that *firms' investment behaviour is influenced by perceptions of quantity constraints in the consumption good market.*

In discussing what I termed the Ricardo case in Chapter 6 I said that even with a rigid real wage a technical-change-induced reduction in employment will be temporary, as the capital accumulation process (also induced by the technical change) proceeds thus increasing demand for labour. I was able to make this statement whilst assuming a fixed real wage because the analysis remained (in that chapter) within a neoclassical conceptual framework in regarding firms as always fully utilising their capacity and then using the resulting profit for investment. In this framework the possibility of excess supply in the consumption good market, or overcapacity, is not allowed (at least given the rest of the assumptions made for both Chapters 6 and 7). In a neo-Keynesian framework of the sort utilised in the present chapter, on the other hand, firms will invest an amount dependent on their expectation of the future level of transactions in the consumption good market; this then determines everything else in the system. It may well imply that the resulting effective aggregate demand is insufficient to support the full utilisation of the firms' current capacity, that is, excess supply may appear in the consumption good market. This fundamental difference is responsible for the divergence of results of the last two chapters.

APPENDIX 1: THE CASE OF UNCERTAIN SALES CONSTRAINTS

Even within the context of quantity-constraint analysis, the model presented in Chapter 7 suffers from a serious defect. Given that in disequilibrium firms will wish to forecast future demand, they are unlikely to base their investment on expectations of consumer demand that are based solely on the level of sales experienced in the previous period. As a consequence of making this assumption, the expected profitability of investment is not allowed to influence current investment demand. It is as a result of this that productive capacity never rises above its *old* Walrasian equilibrium value following the innovation.

In this appendix I will assume that firms are uncertain about future consumption demand but retain the assumptions concerning technology of Chapter 7. Capacity will now attain its new Walrasian equilibrium level; still the problem of persistent Keynesian unemployment, with increasing unemployment and excess capacity, remains. Indeed my main purpose in this appendix is to show that more realistic hypotheses concerning demand *expectations* will not alter the main predictions of the previous model, in the presence of short-run price and wage inflexibility, *and* under the assumption that firms' investment behaviour is governed by perceptions of possibly facing quantity constraints in the consumption good market.

I will use the cumulative distribution function $F(x)$ to represent the probability that is at present attributed by the firms to the event that in the future (period $t + 1$) demand will be less than x. Assuming that firms can obtain an unlimited amount of finance at a fixed rate r, and static expectations concerning the real wage, this means that demand for machines, K_t^d, in period t must now satisfy the following equation:

$$[1 - (w/p)_t a_c] [1 - F(K_t^d)] = (w/p)_t a_k(1 + r) . \quad \text{(A1)}$$

I assume that current profit consumption equals last period's actual profit payments, the latter being the difference between the value of consumption output and wage payments.[7]

In this case the Walrasian equilibrium is defined by the full employment condition $X = L/(a_c + a_k)$ and the condition that the real wage equates the *expected* return to the actual cost of machine; that is, from (A1), $w/p = 1/(a_c + a_k f)$

where $f = \dfrac{1 + r}{1 - F[L/(a_c + a_k)]}$.

Note that profit income is then

$$(w/p)a_k X[r + fF(X)] = X - (w/p)L$$

where $(w/p)a_k XfF(X) = X[1 - (w/p)a_c] - X(1 - w/p)a_c] [1 - F(X)]$, that is, actual minus expected profit on X machines.[8]

Working with (A1) makes the analysis, following the technical change, much more complicated than before; I simplify by assuming a neutral change (so that a_c and a_k are reduced in the same proportion). As before I assume that labour supply to construction and utilisation equals the original Walrasian equilibrium values of L^k and L^c.

In the first perod $(w/p)_1 = (w/p)_0$. Consider the value, K_1' of K_1^d that satisfies:

$$[1 - (w/p)a'_c] [1 - F(K'_1)] = (w/p)_1 \, a'_k \, (1 + r) \; .$$

The first thing to note is that K'_1 will now exceed $X^s_1 = K_0$, that is, machine construction and hence (period 2) capacity will definitely increase above their old Walrasian equilibrium values: the increased profitability of investment must lead to an increase in optimal capacity before it becomes compensated by a reduced likelihood that there will be sufficient demand for this capacity to be fully utilised.

We must then distinguish between two cases:

Case 1: $K'_1 < L^k/a'_k \Rightarrow K_1 = K'_1,$

$$L^{k,e}_1 = a'_k K_1 < L^k = L^{k,e}_0 \; .$$

In this case, with profit consumption in period 1 equal to $X_0 - (w/p)_0 L = X^s_1 - (w/p)_1 \, L$, a Keynesian temporary equilibrium will be established, as with the previous model, the reduction in constructional employment leading to a reduction in effective consumption demand (from wage income) and hence reduction in labour employed in machine utilisation. This may be described more appropriately than would be the case with the previous model, as the case of *'investment pessimism'*. This now means that the probability of demand exceeding capacity falls very rapidly, as current investment increases capacity, thus soon compensating the stimulating effect on investment demand of the technical-change-induced improvement in profitability.

Output in period 1 being $X_1 = profit + (w/p)_1 L^e_1 = X^s_1 - (w/p)_1 \, (L - L^e_1)$, profit in period 1 (= profit consumption in period 2) $= X_1 - (w/p)_1 \, L^e_1$, equals profit in period 0.[9] Unemployment in period 1 means that $(w/p_2 < (w/p)_1$, with $X^s_2 = K_1$. Assume, a case sooner or later to be realised, that the reduction in the real wage leads, in period 2, to an investment demand that is sufficient to absorb L^k, that is, $a'_k K^d_2 \geqslant L^k \Rightarrow L^{k,e} = L^k$. Note that notional consumption demand is, in period 2, equal to $(profit \ consumption)_2 + (w/p)_2 L = X^s_1 - (w/p)_1 L + (w/p)_2 L = X^s_1 - L((w/p)_1 - (w/p)_2) < X^s_1 < X^s_2$. Hence, the excess supply of the consumer good leads to unemployment of utilisational labour. If we make the usual assumption[10] that reductions in the real wage reduce the *aggregate effective* demand for labour, consumption output and employment are reduced in period 2 below their period 1 levels. This in turn leads to a further reduction in w/p in period 3, which again stimulates investment but depresses consumption demand, thus further reducing consumption output and aggregate employment, etc. That is, again, as in the previous case examined in Chapter 7, we get instability with ever increasing unemployment.

Case 2: $K_1^l \geqslant L^k/a_k^l$, $L_1^{k,d'} > L^k$.

In this case $L_1^{k,e} = L^k$. There is, in period 1, full employment and full capacity utilisation. Assume that in period 2 the real wage increases just enough to eliminate any excess demand for constructional labour. That is, in period 2, capacity ($= L^k/a_k^l$) is at its new Walrasian equilibrium level, and the real wage is at the level that just induces firms to employ all constructional labour, that is, build again L^k/a_k^l machines (i.e., the real wage is also at its new Walrasian equilibrium level). On the other hand, profit consumption in period 2, equal to profit income in period 1 ($= X_1^s - (w/p)_1 L =$ profit in old Walrasian equilibrium) is less than its new Walrasian equilibrium level.[11] Notional consumption demand is therefore less than supply—there is excess supply of the consumption good. This leads to excess capacity ($X_2 < L^k/a_k^l$), and unemployment of labour employed in machine utilisation. This, in turn, leads to a reduction of the real wage in period 3. This, plus the fact that profit in period 2 ($X_2 - (w/p)_2 L_2^e = (w/p)_2 L_2^e + (profit)_1 - (w/p)_2 L_2^e$), is equal to profit in period 1, leads to a further reduction in output and employment in period 3, as in case 1, etc.

Note that in this, unlike all previous cases, Keynesian unemployment first appears in period 2 (rather than period 1). Further, in this, unlike previous cases, the immediate cause of unemployment is *not* that firms are 'investment pessimists'. Rather it is that now profit consumption remains low when capacity and the real wage have moved to their new equilibrium levels. The same result would have been obtained if instead we had assumed that firms paid at the beginning of period 2 *expected* profit from full capacity utilisation *but* the increase in profit was *not wholly* consumed in the same period.

APPENDIX 2: TECHNICAL CHANGE AND EMPLOYMENT WHEN DEMAND CURVES ARE KINKED

In Chapter 7 it was *assumed* that prices were fixed in the short run. In this appendix I will deal briefly with a way of dispensing with the fixprice assumption, which has especially interesting implications when considered in the context of an analysis of the employment effects of technical change. This is based on the idea of imperfect information and, as already mentioned, has been recently utilised by Negishi (1979) in an attempt to provide microfoundations to Keynesian macroeconomics. Negishi's approach has been more successful in explaining price, rather than wage, stickiness. Below, rather than considering a complete general equilibrium model, I summarize the main concepts of this approach as applied to firm behaviour, in order to gain an insight about its relevance to our own main concerns.

Negishi utilises the concept of 'perceived demand functions'. These may be formulated by first taking as given a starting point, denoted by $\bar{p}$ and X, the realised price and sale respectively.

When the realised starting point is given, i.e. the firm finds that $\bar{X}$ is currently being sold at price $\bar{p}$, the firm perceives a subjective or imaginary inverse demand function, $p = p(X, \bar{p}, X)$, where X is the possible level of sales and p is the price at which X can be expected to be cleared. This function must be consistent with the given information on the present state of the market $\bar{p} = p(X, \bar{p}, X)$, i.e. the perceived demand curve must pass through the starting point. On the basis of this function, the firm calculates p and X which are expected to produce the maximum profits. Generally however this p and X cannot be realised. Then the firm modifies its perceived demand curve on the basis of a new starting point. The equilibrium is the situation in which the profit expected on the basis of the perceived demand function is maximised at the starting point on which the demand function is perceived.[12]

Now, a competitive firm's perceived demand curve will

generally have kinks in a non-Walrasian monetary exchange economy where information is not perfect. This is due to the assymetric reaction of customers.... Lower prices asked by a supplier may not be fully advertised to customers currently buying from other suppliers who are maintaining their current price, while a higher price charged by the same supplier necessarily induces present customers to leave in search of lower price suppliers.

Further, a competitive firm cannot exceed 'the current price given in the market and therefore the perceived demand curve is infinitely elastic for a level of sales lower than the current level, though not for a level higher than the current one.'[13]

To simplify, I now relax the assumption utilised in Chapters 6 and 7 that it takes one period to construct a machine; instead I assume that the machine can be produced instantaneously (and lasts for a period). '*a*' will denote the amount of labour required to construct and utilise a machine, so that the firm's marginal (and average) production cost is wa.

Suppose the starting point of the *i*th competitive firm is given as $(\bar{p}_i, X_i)$ where $\bar{p}_i$ denotes the current market price of the output of the *i*th firm and X_i denotes its current sales. Since the firm is prevented by competition from exceeding the current price and realises the difficulty of selling a large quantity without a reduction in price, it perceives a demand curve through the starting point of a demand function $p_i = p_i(X_i, \bar{p}_i, X_i)$ such that $\bar{p}_i = \bar{p}_i(X_i, \bar{p}_i, X_i)$ and that $p_i = \bar{p}_i$ for $X_i \leq X_i$ and $\partial p_i/\partial X_i < 0$ for $X_i > X_i$, where X_i is the possible level of output and p_i is the price at which X_i can be sold.[14] The profit of the firm, to be maximised, is given as $p_i(X_i, \bar{p}_i, X_i)(L_i/a) - wL_i$ where L_i denotes the input of labour service. When the short-term expectation is realised, that is $X_i = X_i$, and therefore $p_i = \bar{p}_i$, the conditions for maximisation are:

$$p_i(1 - e_i) \leq wa \qquad (A2)$$

$$p_i \geq wa \qquad (A3)$$

at $(\bar{p}_i, \bar{X}_i)$ where e_i is the right-hand side elasticity of p_i with respect to X_i at $X_i = \bar{X}_i$.[15]

Conditions (A2) and (A3) imply that the marginal cost is no larger than the price and no smaller than the marginal revenue $p_i(1 - e_i)$ for any increase in the level of output. Estimation of the perceived demand function and maximisation of the profit will be repeated as long as conditions (A2) and (A3) are not satisfied at the starting point. Once they are satisfied, however, the firm is at a Keynesian conjectural equilibrium since its short-term expectation has been realised, but there is no incentive for the firm to change the price or level of output, even though that price will be generally higher than marginal cost.

Consider now the case where at given w, the labour that firms wish to employ at this conjectural equilibrium is less than (or equal to) labour supply. When inequalities (A2) and (A3) are satisfied in the inequality form, small changes in the parameter a will leave them, and hence the equilibrium price and output, undisturbed; whilst then, firms will wish to employ less labour to produce their equilibrium output. Hence, process innovation leading to small reductions in the labour coefficient will lead to increased unemployment. Slight changes in w will not affect this result. When, on the other hand, the level of effective demand increases, sales can be increased by increasing output and employment, without any change in price.

NOTES

1. J.M. Grandmont 'The logic of the fixprice method', p. 23; in Strom and Werin (1978). For an excellent survey *see* Malinvaud (1977), or the more recent Fitoussi 'Modern macroeconomic theory: an overview' in Fitoussi (1983).
2. H.R. Varian 'The stability of a disequilibrium IS–LM model', p. 115; in Strom and Werin (1978).
3. In Appendix 2 I follow Negishi's argument in his *Microeconomic Foundations of Keynesian Macroeconomics* (1979). The implications of cost-reducing technical change when the monopolistically competitive industry is at a 'kinked equilibrium' are similar to those (examined in Appendix 2) that arise when kinked demand curves are due to imperfect information.
4. One could alternatively assume that a one-period lag is required for labour employed in one sector to be transferred to the other sector; such transfer would take place if, relative

to the previous period's labour allocation, there was now an excess demand for labour in one, and an excess supply in the other sector. Such transfers are not required for the analysis of this section, as demand for labour in both sectors will always be below the initial Walrasian equilibrium allocation of labour to the two sectors.

5. It will not if the reduction in capacity, starting with period 3, is less than the reduction in notional consumption demand. Below I obtain sufficient conditions for this.

6. Since $L_{t-1}^{d'} = L_{t-1}^{k,e} + L_{t-1}^{c,e} = L_{t-2}^{e}$.

7. *Cf.* Varian, *ab. cit.* p. 118.

8. As Malinvaud notes, 'there may seem to be an element of contradiction between the two hypotheses that a stationary equilibrium is achieved but that firms' decisions are essentially dependent on uncertainties about the future.

   Once again, it must be remembered that we do not want to study here long-term growth, but only the dynamic links between short-term equilibria..... The stationary Walrasian equilibrium ... [must be considered] as a simple and useful characteristic of a formal model for the study of medium term dynamics. In these circumstances it is admissible to consider as given the type and degree of uncertainty that the firms consider as affecting their future activity' (*ab. cit.* pp. 38–9).

9. Since $X_1 = (profit)_0 + (w/p)_1 L_1^e = X_1^s - (w/p)_1 (L - L_1^e)$; hence, $X_1^s - X_1 = (w/p)_1 (L - L_1^e)$; hence, $(profit)_1 = X_1 - (w/p)_1 L_1^e = (profit)_0 = X_1^s - (w/p)_1 L$.

10. *See* for example, Barro and Grossman (1976), pp. 61–2, or Malinvaud, *ab. cit.* p. 45.

11. There is an increase in profit between the new and old Walrasian equilibrium, as can be seen by writing profit as the difference between the levels of output and wage income in the two equilibria. Profit in new equilibrium is $L/(a_c' + a_k') - L/(a_c' + a_k'f')$ where $f' = (1 + r)/\{1 - F[L/(a_c' + a_k')]\}$ whilst profit in old equilibrium was $L/(a_c + a_k) - L/(a_c + a_kf)$ where $f = (1 + r)\{1 - F[L/(a_c + a_k)]\}$.

12. Negishi, T. *ab. cit.* pp. 81–2; Chamberlin's *dd* curve is an example of a perceived demand function and is discussed by Negishi in pp. 78–9.

13. *ibid.* p. 87.

14. Negishi, T., *ab. cit.* p. 89.

15. *ibid.*, pp. 89–90.

8 Technical Change and Structural Unemployment

8.1 THE STRUCTURALIST THESIS: A REVIEW AND INTRODUCTION

Up to this point I have consistently treated labour as a homogeneous factor of production. In this chapter I will drop this assumption and assume that labour is heterogeneous. My main purpose is to illustrate the conditions under which technical change leads to structural unemployment. The inclusion here of the following analysis seems to be justified by a number of considerations:

(a) It enables one to focus on the *structural* unemployment-creating effect of technical change. Whilst the structuralist thesis has been a very important part of the debate on the cause of rising unemployment at the beginning of the 1960s and at present, no formal analytical examination of this thesis has been produced.

(b) By providing such an examination, and by comparison with the analysis of Chapter Six, we are able to answer the following question: is it more likely for technical change to have adverse 'structural', as opposed to adverse 'general', effects on employment? The following analysis suggests an affirmative answer to this question.

(c) The policy implications of the general as opposed to the structural effects of technical change are not the same.

Structural unemployment may be defined, at an abstract level, as 'the qualitative mismatch of the demand for labour and the supply of workers'. The term is usually confusingly used to describe groups of workers that are thought to be unemployed because:

(a) they lack the skills required for available jobs;
(b) there has been a change in the industrial structure of employment, due to a changing composition of final demand;
(c) there is a geographical mismatch between the demand for and the supply of labour;
(d) of demographic shifts.[1]

However, unemployment that arises due to factors (b), (c) and (d) must actually be caused either because of a mismatch of skills (that is, factor (a)), or is *frictional* (that is, caused by labour immobility between sectors or geographical regions). Hence, the term structural unemployment will be used below to refer only to those workers that are thought to be unemployed because they lack the required skills.

Indeed, the 'structural unemployment thesis', which gained prominence in USA in the first part of the 1960s, and which was eclipsed after the publication of Solow's Wicksell Lectures in 1964 (demonstrating that there was very little empirical evidence to validate this thesis)[2] and has resurfaced recently, relied on a distinction between 'skilled' and 'unskilled' workers to argue that much of the rising unemployment in the western industrialised world was due to a relative decline in opportunities for the unskilled group of workers owing to technological progress. The most prominent of the original exponents of this thesis, C. Killingworth, writing in 1963 about post-war structural change in the United States, argued that:

despite some exceptions, it seems justifiable to generalise that the displacement impact of structural change fell first at the bottom of the skill and educational attainment ladder but in more recent years began to reach into the middle levels. At the upper end of the skill and educational attainment ladder, structural change has contributed heavily to the growth of demand. In a remarkably broad range of industries, the employment of higher skilled non-production workers has grown while the employment of lower skilled production workers has grown much more slowly or has actually declined.[3]

It is now easy to see how technical change may reduce the demand for labour for one group of workers, in the case of *fixed production coefficients*. Consider first the extreme case, depicted in Figure 8.1 below, where production is initially at X_0, with fixed coefficients, and will full employment of L_s^s and L_u^s units of skilled and unskilled labour. The technical change makes it possible to produce the same output with less of each factor at X_0'. However, it also biases the ratio in which factors may be used in production, saving more unskilled than skilled labour. Accordingly, output can now only follow the expansion path OY'; maximum output and employment is reached at X_1' where all skilled labour has been employed. This leaves a structural unemployment of $L_u^s - L_u'$ of unskilled labour, which cannot be reduced by factor price shifts.

Now turn to a rather more relevant variation of this case. Assume that *two goods* are produced, with fixed coefficients, but of different skill intensity. Assume that good B has a

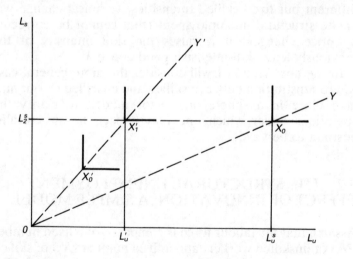

Figure 8.1

lower skill intensity than good A, and denote these intensities by j_A and j_B, respectively. It may be shown that it is necessary for full employment that

$$j_A > (L_s^s/L_u^s) > j_B .$$ (1)

This can be as seen as follows: full employment requires that

$$\frac{L_s^s}{L_u^s} = \frac{n_A X_A + n_B X_B}{m_A X_A + m_B X_B}$$ (2)

where n_A and n_B (m_A and m_B) are the skilled (unskilled) labour required per unit of A and B output, respectively. Solving for X_A/X_B we obtain:

$$\frac{X_A}{X_B} = - \frac{m_A}{m_B} \left(\frac{\lambda - j_B}{\lambda - j_A} \right)$$ (3)

where $\lambda = L_s^s/L_u^s$. For this to be positive, inequality (1) must hold. If technical change raises the skill intensity in both sectors and makes that of sector B greater than λ then 'pure' structural unemployment again results (as in the one-sector case). This story may be told for any number of goods of different but fixed skilled intensities: technical change will create structural unemployment (that cannot be corrected by price changes) if it raises the skill intensity of the previously least skill-intensive good above λ.[4]

In the next section I will consider the more general case where substitution between skilled and unskilled labour may take place in a simple one-sector model, to clarify the conditions under which one may expect the structuralist position to be valid.

8.2   THE STRUCTURAL UNEMPLOYMENT EFFECT OF INNOVATION: A SIMPLE MODEL

Assume that the labour force is composed of a fixed number (N_u) of unskilled workers and a fixed number (N_s) of skilled workers—assumed to be non-competing groups.[5] The workers are the only consumers, their consumption–leisure choice, in any given period, being the outcome of:

$$\max\ U(X,\ K - k)\ \text{s.t.}\ wk = pX,$$

where U is a utility function with the usual properties, K is the number of time units in a period, k the number of units supplied for work, and p the output price. Assume, for simplicity, that this maximisation results in each worker supplying a number of labour units per period that is invariant to the level of the real wage. That is, the labour supply decision of worker i is as shown in Figure 8.2. If it is further assumed that a worker is entitled to unemployment benefit, that is such that the worker is guaranteed a real income of X per period, the supply of labour decision of worker i may be described as in Figure 8.3, where $(\bar{w}/p)$ is defined by $(w/p)\bar{k}_i = X$.

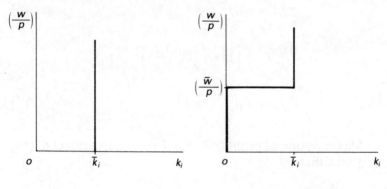

Figure 8.2   Figure 8.3

Let L_u^s and L_s^s denote the fixed aggregate supply of unskilled and skilled labour units, respectively, per period, where:

$$L_u^s = \sum_{i=1}^{N_u} k_{i,u} \quad \text{and} \quad L_s^s = \sum_{i=1}^{N_s} k_{i,s}. \tag{4}$$

On the production side, I now assume that output X is produced by a CES production function:

$$X = T[\delta_s(A_sL_s)^{\sigma-1/\sigma} + \delta_u(A_uL_u)^{\sigma-1/\sigma}]^{\sigma/\sigma-1} \qquad (5)$$

where δ_s, δ_u are constants ($\delta_s = 1 - \delta_u$), T is a Hicks-neutral technology parameter, σ is the elasticity of substitution and A_s, A_u are technology parameters, registering, when raised, skilled and unskilled labour-augmenting technological progress.

One may obtain:

$$MP_i = \frac{\partial X}{\partial L_i} = A_i\delta_iT^{\sigma-1/\sigma}\left[\frac{X}{A_iL_i}\right]^{1/\sigma}$$

$$= A_iT\delta_i^{\sigma/\sigma-1}\left[1 + \left(\frac{\delta_j}{\delta_i}\right)\left(\frac{A_jL_j}{A_iL_i}\right)^{\sigma-1/\sigma}\right]^{1/\sigma-1};$$

$$j,i = s,u; \quad j \ne i \qquad (6)$$

$$s_i = \frac{MP_iL_i}{X} = \left[1 + \left(\frac{\delta_j}{\delta_i}\right)\left(\frac{A_jL_j}{A_iL_i}\right)^{\sigma-1/\sigma}\right]^{-1};$$

$$j,i = s,u; \quad j \ne i. \qquad (7)$$

Maximisation of profit ($pX - w_sL_s - w_uL_u$) subject to (5), requires that:

$$MP_s = w_s/p \quad \text{and} \quad MP_u = w_u/p \qquad (8)$$

Solving equations (8) by using equations (6) gives the profit-maximising levels of L_s and L_u. These are given by

$$L_u = \frac{\delta_s^{\sigma/\sigma-1}\delta_u^\sigma T^\sigma A_u^{\sigma-1}A_sL_s}{[(w_u/p)^{\sigma-1} - A_u^{\sigma-1}\delta_u^\sigma T^{\sigma-1}]^{\sigma/\sigma-1}} \qquad (9)$$

and

$$L_s = \frac{\delta_u^{\sigma/\sigma-1}\delta_s^\sigma T^\sigma A_s^{\sigma-1}A_uL_u}{[(w_s/p)^{\sigma-1} - A_s^{\sigma-1}\delta_s^\sigma T^{\sigma-1}]^{\sigma/\sigma-1}}. \qquad (10)$$

In Walrasian equilibrium,

$$L_u = L_u^s \quad \text{and} \quad L_s = L_s^s , \tag{11}$$

that is, labour markets must clear. Substituting equations (11) into (9) and (10), and solving, gives the values of wages that will clear the labour markets.

We may now use equations (9) and (10) to obtain relationships between the technical change parameters and variations in the profit-maximising input levels, for given real wage rates. The proportional variation in L_u and L_s may be obtained by total differentiation of (9) and (10) respectively, account being taken of equations (7), which may also be written as follows:

$$s_i = \frac{(A_i T)^{\sigma-1} \delta_i^\sigma}{(w_i/p)^{\sigma-1}}; \quad i = s,u . \tag{7'}$$

It may then be seen that:

$$\frac{dL_u}{L_u} = \frac{\sigma}{s_s} \frac{dT}{T} + \frac{dA_u}{A_u}\left(\frac{\sigma}{s_s} - 1\right) + \frac{dA_s}{A_s} + \frac{dL_s}{L_s} \tag{12}$$

and

$$\frac{dL_s}{L_s} = \frac{\sigma}{s_u} \frac{dT}{T} + \frac{dA_s}{A_s}\left(\frac{\sigma}{s_u} - 1\right) + \frac{dA_u}{A_u} + \frac{dL_u}{L_u} . \tag{13}$$

Hence, demand for unskilled labour at any given real wage rate of this labour *and* given skilled labour input ($dL_s = 0$) will:

(a) increase under only Hicks-neutral technical change ($dA_u = dA_s = 0$);

(b) increase under only skilled labour-augmenting technical change ($dT = dA_u = 0$);

(c) increase under only unskilled labour-augmenting technical change ($dT = dA_s = 0$), *iff* $\sigma > s_s$.

Alternatively, if the proportional changes in T, A_u and A_s are g,m and n per cent per period, dL_u/L_u will be positive provided

$$\frac{\sigma}{s_s} (g + m) > m - n \tag{14}$$

whilst dL_s/L_s will be positive provided

$$\frac{\sigma}{s_u} (g + n) > n - m \ . \tag{15}$$

One may interpret the structuralist thesis as implying that $m > n$, in which case (15) certainly holds—there is a growth in the demand for skilled labour. On the other hand, unskilled labour-augmenting technological progress at a rate greater than skilled labour-augmenting technological progress (i.e., $m > n$) is not sufficient for a reduction in demand for unskilled labour. In particular, demand will increase under these conditions provided the elasticity of substitution, σ, between skilled and unskilled labour is sufficiently high. If, on the other hand, this is not so, and there *is* a decline in the demand for unskilled labour, a Walrasian equilibrium will be sustained only if the real wage of unskilled labour declines (whilst that of skilled labour is increased). Assuming that absolute and relative wages are flexible in both directions, voluntary unemployment of unskilled labour may still result in the presence of unemployment benefit payments. For consider a worker with labour supply as depicted in Figure 8.3 above who is initially fully employed—that is, supplying $\bar{k}$ units of labour per period. Were the reduction in demand for his services to be such that at $(\bar{w}/p)$—Figure 8.3—he can now supply an amount of labour units that is less than $\bar{k}$, he will prefer to remain less than fully employed rather than bid down the wage rate. In the situation shown in Figure 8.4 below, technical change has reduced demand for unskilled labour to the point indicated by L_u^d; employment equals demand, at L_u, and we will observe an amount of unemployment of $L_u^s - L_u$ that is voluntary. (In this figure it is assumed that all unskilled workers supply the same fixed number of labour units per period, $\bar{k}$, so that $L_u^s = \bar{k}N_u$.)

8.3 CONCLUDING REMARKS

To conclude, let us first return to the assumption (noted at the beginning of section 8.2) that skilled and unskilled

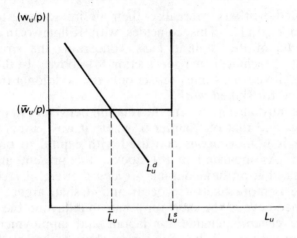

Figure 8.4

workers constitute non-competing groups. Since training requires time this is a proper assumption for the analysis of the *short- or medium-run* structural unemployment effect of technical change.

Thus, the above analysis indicates that, in the short or medium run, when the proportion of skilled to unskilled workers may be treated as constant, technical change will reduce the demand for unskilled labour if the technical change is relatively more unskilled labour augmenting *and* the elasticity of substitution between skilled and unskilled labour is sufficiently low. Employment of unskilled labour may then be reduced in the presence of unemployment insurance. (Of course, this will also occur in the presence of wage inflexibility).

The assumption that skilled and unskilled labour are non-competing is less appropriate for long-run analysis. Under conditions of relatively more unskilled-labour-augmenting technological progress—and hence of a rising real wage of skilled relative to unskilled labour—more and more unskilled workers will come to consider extra training the most attractive alternative. Hence, *the proportion of skilled to unskilled workers in employment will be rising over time,* if it is assumed that it is feasible in the long run for unskilled workers to realise their desire in investing in human capital.[6] (This coincides with Killingworth's presentation of the 'stylised facts' concerning the structural impact of technical change—section 8.1 above.) In the long run, relative wages must reflect only the additional training required for skilled work.

One must also note here the relation between the present analysis and that of Chapter 6, where it was assumed that labour is homogeneous and used with capital to produce output. As indicated in 8.1 above, the present analysis suggests that an unfavourable *structural* effect of technical change is more likely (to occur and, I shall argue, to be sustained beyond the short run) than an unfavourable effect on the *general* demand for labour and employment. In Chapter 6 I termed the (only) case where technical change has an unfavourable short-run impact on labour demand the 'Ricardo case'. As was noted there, this is the result of a short-run capital shortage that is reversed—*even with the real wage fixed*—as the improved profitability associated with the introduction of innovation induces a process of capital accumulation. It is also clear that *even in the short run* the reduction in labour demand would not take place were firms able to increase their capital stock. As Hicks suggests in *Capital and Time*,[7] the Ricardo case has empirical relevance only to the extent that less developed countries, lacking foreign exchange to import capital (*and* with near to subsistence wage levels), introduce strongly capital-using technological improvements that reduce aggregate labour demand.

On the other hand, if technical change reduces demand for unskilled labour, the only way in which one would avoid either a reduction in the real wage of this labour or a reduction in its employment would be retraining, and the latter does require sometimes a considerable period of time. The existence of imperfections in the capital and labour markets makes things worse. In their presence, the government would help to alleviate the technical-change-induced structural unemployment by pursuing so-called labour market policies (e.g., instituting retraining schemes) that may speed up the increase in the proportion of skilled labour in the labour force. (Of course, in the presence of wage inflexibility, expansionary fiscal policy may be used to prevent the emergence of involuntary unskilled-labour unemployment.)

My overall conclusion must be that in an examination of the general versus the structural effects of technological progress, the fact that it may be easier in the short and medium run to raise the physical rather than the human capital stock is the most important differentiating aspect.[8]

NOTES

1. The above are taken from a recent review by Standing (1983).
2. In Rothwell and Zegveld (1979), p. 2, the authors write: 'On the whole the predominant view in the debate (in the 1960s) was that the unemployment problem in the USA was overwhelmingly one of demand, rather than one of the structural or technical change'. The same authors provide a 'structuralist' interpretation of the contemporary unemployment problem in Chapter 11 of *Industrial Innovation and Public Policy* (1981). This is challenged in Layard *et àl.* (1984); the latter find no evidence that structural unemployment has become more severe since the early 1970s in the major European economies.
3. 'Structural unemployment in the United States' in Siebert (ed.), (1966).
4. The above analysis is included in Clark and Cooper (1982).
5. I will return to this assumption in the concluding section of this chapter.
6. That is, if it is assumed that there are no impediments from imperfections in the capital and labour markets.
7. Page 99.
8. Finally, one should note here that above I have examined only one (the most well known) of the competing hypotheses concerning the impact of technical change on the skill composition of the labour force. In following this (i.e., the structuralist approach) I have treated labour as divided into skill categories. These refer to different amounts of training that are required to perform different tasks that are all essential in a particular process. There is, however, a quite different view. The wider issue of the employment effect of technical change on the

division of labour may be approached in another way. This approach would regard 'skills' as referring to differential productivities in performing a particular task and would consider technical change as primarily acting so as to eliminate these differences (usually via the introduction of more sophisticated capital equipment) thereby increasing the effective supply of *'skilled'* labour. On this view and relevant evidence see Standing, *ab. cit.* p. 140 and the references cited there.

9 Summary and Conclusions

As was noted in the introductory chapter, despite the long-standing interest of economists (which goes back to Ricardo) on the possible effects of technological progress on the labour market, very few formal theoretical works were produced on the subject until very recently. To quote again from a recent work:

From the Luddites of the early nineteenth century to the Clive Jenkinses of the late twentieth, a crucial economic and therefore political and sociological question has been whether technical progress, broadly defined, causes unemployment. But little has been done to answer this question within the framework of economic theory.[1]

The present book is intended as a further contribution in this area, the practical significance of which has increased enormously over the last few years, during which we have witnessed increasingly high levels of unemployment accompanied by the introduction of major new technological advances.

My approach to the study of the employment effect of technical change was to rely, for the most part of my investigations, on equilibrium economic theory in order to discover the way in which technical change affects the demand for and supply of labour. As a preliminary to a more detailed discussion of the conclusions of my analysis one may first note that the results do not seem to justify Kaldor's and Hicks' somewhat exaggerated optimism, recorded in the

149

introductory chapter and based on informal theorising about the impact of *process* innovation on the labour market. Whether one looks at the matter from a partial or from a general equilibrium viewpoint, my conclusions do not justify Kaldor's remark that 'the optimistic conclusions regarding the effects of innovation following self-evidently from the general notions of the theory of equilibrium and, therefore, do not seem to demand a special proof'.

However, I did not just deal with the impact effect of process innovation. The investigations of this book have revolved around two major themes. The first, which was explored in Part One, was based on the empirical distinction between process and product innovation which (as I noted many times above) has been prominent in much of the recent empirical literature on the employment effect of technical change. In this respect the present work provides for the first time theoretical support for the often-quoted empirical observation that the impact of product innovation on employment is more likely to be favourable than is the impact on employment of process innovation. I showed that, whilst both process and product innovation raise the full employment ceiling, that is, the level of employment that can be attained by expansionary government policy at each level of the wage rate, for process innovation the *impact effect* may be a reduction in the level of employment, whilst for product innovation even the impact effect involves a rise in the level of employment (where I mean by impact effect the short-run effect with nominal aggregate expenditure fixed).

To be more specific, my main findings in Part One may be conveniently summarised under the following headings (corresponding to Chapters 2–5).

A. The short-run partial equilibrium effect of process innovation

(a) A competitive industry's demand for labour will be reduced at given real wages if the technical change is Hicksian labour saving and the short-run price elasticity of output supply is less than unity; its demand for labour at given nominal wages will be reduced if the elasticity of demand is less than unity, for Hicks-neutral technical change.

(b) When the demand schedule is of constant elasticity, market structure has no influence on the way technical change affects labour demand. If it is of increasing (decreasing) elasticity, the likelihood that technical change increases labour demand (i.e., $\hat{L} > 0$) is greater (smaller) the more monopolistic the market structure. For given market structure, the likelihood that $\hat{L} > 0$ is greater the greater is the elasticity of demand and the greater (smaller) is the absolute value of the elasticity of elasticity when this is positive (negative). The elasticity of substitution between labour and capital, the extent of technological progress and the value of the labour share in total cost have no influence on the sign of $\hat{L}$ when technical change is Hicks neutral, whilst the greater (smaller) their value the more likely it is that $\hat{L}$ will be positive due to labour(capital)-saving technical change.

(c) Cost-reducing process innovation will reduce the amount of labour employed in a short-run temporary Keynesian equilibrium.

B. The short-run general equilibrium effect of process innovation

(a) By reducing prices and thus increasing the workers' utility from consumption relative to disutility from work, cost-reducing process innovation will increase labour supply and thus raise the full employment ceiling.

(b) When the effect of process innovation is balanced (i.e., it reduces the sectors' unit costs equiproportionately), and preferences are homothetic, total labour demand is unaffected.

(c) When the effect of process innovation is sector specific, it may or may not increase aggregate labour demand, depending on which sector is affected by the change. Generally speaking, process innovation increases aggregate labour demand if it leads to a shift in expenditure to the sector where expenditure required to employ a labour unit is least. With one factor, constant returns and homothetic preferences, this will occur if the sector affected by the change is the small share-high elasticity sector. Technical change affecting the large share-low elasticity sector will lead to a reduction in aggregate labour demand. A corollary of these is that process innovation, by reducing the relative price and increasing the relative share of the sector affected by it, will eventually have a negative impact on total labour demand if it persistently affects the same sector, even if its initial impact leads to an increase in this demand.

C. **The general equilibrium effect of product innovation**
   (a) In a monopolistically competitive economy, with products 'horizontally' differentiated, the introduction of a new consumer good will *ceteris paribus*, lead to an increase, in equilibrium, of the workers' welfare and hence to an increase in the amount of labour employed in equilibrium. This I termed the 'welfare effect' of product innovation on employment.
   (b) The increase in the equilibrium level of employment attained as new consumer goods are introduced is smaller the greater is the substitutability between the products. In the limit, as the products become perfect substitutes the effect on the equilibrium level of employment of the introduction of additional products tends to zero. I termed this the 'displacement effect' of product innovation.
   (c) In the Chamberlinian ('horizontal' differentiation) case there is a clear intuitive link between the displacement and the welfare effects of product innovation on employment. The introduction of goods which are close substitutes involves a large 'displacement effect' and a small 'welfare effect', and so has little impact on employment. By considering the 'vertical' differentiation case (i.e., the case where products are differentiated by quality) we were able to see that even when the 'displacement effect' is very large, the employment-creating effect of product innovation

may be significant—all the more so when the introduction of new products by new firms enhances competition and so further raises consumer welfare.

Turning to Part Two of the book, this was concerned with a separate idea: the distinction between flexible and sticky prices in relation to the employment effect of innovation in the long run. My aim was to deal with two major limitations of the analysis of Part One, the first being associated with the assumption of fixed nominal aggregate expenditure. In Part Two I endogenised aggregate expenditure in two contrasting ways: I used a simplified two-sector (producing a consumer and a capital good) model, first under a flexprice assumption and then under a fixprice assumption, to examine the transition path of the economy following process innovation.

In the first case I got convergence to a new full employment Walrasian equilibrium (given the satisfaction of certain stability conditions) whatever the short-run impact of the innovation on labour demand; even though I showed that the path to the new Walrasian equilibrium is not smooth (it involves overshooting) in all but the case where the effect of innovation on the consumer and capital good sectors is the same (i.e., the case of neutral technical change).

In the second case, on the other hand, not only did I get a short-run adverse effect on labour demand (a result that strengthens the one-sector conclusion mentioned above, concerning the impact effect of process innovation on a temporary Keynesian equilibrium), but I found that the long-run equilibrium may exhibit dynamic instability, in the sense that the transition path does not converge to long-run equilibrium but involves ever increasing unemployment. This instability remains a feature of the fixprice analysis under different assumptions concerning expectations, and is rather a result of the assumption that firms' investment behaviour is governed by perceptions of the possibility of future quantity constraints in the consumer good market.

My second concern in Part Two was to study those aspects of technical change repercussions that arise in connection with the process of capital formation, as well as the structural effects of technical change. In doing so I provided a formal treatment of the famous Ricardo case, which involves a short-run reduction in aggregate labour demand as a result of technical change. I noted that this is the result of a short-run capital shortage—I showed that it is reversed, even in the presence of real wage rigidity, by the capital accumulation process induced by the improved profitability that is the result of the introduction of the innovation. On the other hand, any adverse structural effects of technical change on the demand for the unskilled group of workers will not be easily alleviated; this would require an increase in the stock of human capital, a more difficult task than raising the stock of physical capital. The practical significance of this is enhanced in view of the fact that the conditions under which technical change will reduce the demand for unskilled workers—a relatively more unskilled labour-augmenting technological progress and a low elasticity of substitution between skilled and unskilled labour—seem to be those that are likely to be obtained in reality.

Finally, the results of the present study may be unified to provide a coherent theoretical explanation of the aggregate employment effect of innovation over the life-cycle of an industry. The analysis leads to the prediction—that is at least consistent with the Schumpeterian long-wave theory mentioned in the introduction—of a cyclical movement of total labour demand and employment, over the industry's life cycle, as a result of the innovative activity taking place in the industry.

The introduction of new consumer goods, leading to the creation of new industries, will have, according to the analysis of Section B of Part One, a positive impact on the equilibrium level of employment. Furthermore, the period of substantial product improvements and introduction of many new and better varieties that replace previously existing ones, which follows the first commercial application of major innovations, will also be accompanied, according to the analysis of Chapter 5, by a positive employment effect. As the industry develops, apart from product improvements, process innovations that lead to reductions in costs will also take place. However, as Chapter 3 indicates, whilst the industry remains 'small' relative to other industries or sectors producing competing commodities, this will also tend to increase total labour demand and employment. As the industry grows, on the other hand, and its share increases, further process innovation may tend to reduce total labour demand and employment (Chapter 3), especially if it is not accompanied by further product improvements. In this respect one should remember that, as I have already indicated in section 4.1, there is some evidence that an industry attains maturity and starts to decline simultaneously as the importance of product as compared with process innovation for the industry declines.

NOTES

1. Heffernan (1980), p.1.

References

BOOKS AND THESES

Barro, R. and Grossman, H. (1976) *Money, Employment and Inflation* CUP, Cambridge.

Clark, J. and Cooper, C.N. (1982) *Employment, Economics and Technology: the Impact of Technical Change on the Labour Market*, Wheatsheaf, Brighton.

Fitoussi, J.P., (Ed.) (1983) *Modern Macroeconomic Theory*, Basil Blackwell, Oxford.

Freeman, C., Clark, J. and Soete, L. (1982) *Unemployment and Technical Innovation: a Study of Long Waves and Economic Development*, Frances Pinter, London.

Gourvitch, A. (1940) *Survey of the Economic Theory of Technological Change and Employment*, Augustus Kelley, New York, (reprinted, 1966).

Heffernan, S. (1980) 'Technological unemployment', M. Phil. thesis, Oxford.

Hicks, J. (1932) *Theory of Wages*, Macmillan, London.

Hicks, J. (1973) *Capital and Time*, OUP, Oxford.

Hicks, J. (1977) *Economic Perspectives*, OUP, Oxford.

Kierzkowski, H. (Ed.) (1983) *Monopolistic Competition and International Trade*, CUP, Cambridge.

Malinvaud, E. (1977) *The Theory of Unemployment Reconsidered*, Basil Blackwell, Oxford.

——(1980) *Profitability and Unemployment*, CUP, Cambridge.

——and Fitoussi, J.P. (Eds.) (1980) *Unemployment in Western Countries*, International Economic Association.

Morishima, M. (1969) *Theory of Economic Growth*, CUP, Cambridge.

Negishi, T. (1979) *Microfoundations of Keynesian Macroeconomics*, North Holland Publishing Company, Amsterdam.

Pavit, K. (Ed.) (1980) *Technical Innovation and British Economic Performance*, Macmillan, London.

Ricardo, I. (1973) *The Principles of Political Economy and Taxation*, J.M. Dent, London.

Rothwell R., and Zegveld, W. (1979) *Technical Change and Employment*, Frances Pinter, London.

——(1981) *Industrial Innovation and Public Policy*, Macmillan, London.

Schumpeter, J. (1934) *The Theory of Economic Development*, OUP, Oxford (German edition, 1912).

——(1939) *Business Cycles*, (two volumes), McGraw Hill, Maidenhead, Berks.

Siebert, J. (Ed.) (1966) *Employment Problems of Automation and Advanced Technology*, Macmillan, London.

Solow, R. (1964) *The Nature and Sources of Unemployment in USA*, Wicksell Lectures, Almqvist and Wiksell, Stockholm.

Stoneman, P. (1976) *Technological Diffusion and the Computer Revolution*, CUP, Cambridge.

——(1983) *The Economic Analysis of Technological Change*, OUP, Oxford.

——et al, (1984) *Out of Work*, Department of Economics, University of Warwick.

Strom, S. and Werin, L. (Eds.) (1978) *Topics in Disequilibrium Economics*, Macmillan, London.

ARTICLES

Abernathy, W.J. and Utterback, J.M. (1978) 'Patterns of industrial innovation', *Technology Review*, **80**.

Blattner, N. (1979) 'On some well-known theoretical propositions on the employment effects of technical change', published in *Schweiz. Nationalfonds, Nationales Forschungsprogram 'Regional Problems', Informations*—Bulletin der Programmleitung, No. 2, Bern.

Dixit, A. and Stiglitz, J. (1977) 'Monopolistic competition and optimal product diversity', *American Economic Review*, June, pp. 297–308.

Dobbs, I.M., Hill, M.B. and Waterson, M. (1983) 'Industrial structure and the employment consequences of technical change', mimeo, University of Newcastle-upon-Tyne.

158   *References*

Douglas, P.H. (1930) 'Technological unemployment', *American Federationist*.

Frey, B. (1969) 'Product and process innovation in economic growth', *Zeitschrift für Nationaloconomie*, **29**, pp. 29–38.

Gabszewicz, J.J. and Thisse, J.F. (1980) 'Entry (and exit) in a differentiated industry', *Journal of Economic Theory*, **22**, pp. 327–38.

Gabszewicz, J.J., Shaked, A., Sutton, J. and Thisse, J.F. (1981) 'International trade in differentiated products', *International Economic Review*, **22**, pp. 527–34.

——(1982) 'Segmenting the market: the monopolist's optimal product mix', Core Discussion Paper No. 8242.

Grandmont, J.M. (1978) 'The logic of the fixprice method' in *Topics in Disequilibrium Economics* Strom, S. and Werin, L. (Eds.), Macmillan, London.

Hansen, A. (1931) 'Institutional frictions and technological unemployment', *Quarterly Journal of Economics*, **XLV**, p. 684.

——(1932) 'The theory of technological progress and dislocation of employment', *American Economic Review*, **XLIV**.

Kaldor, N. (1932) 'A case against technical progress', *Economica*, p. 180.

Kamien, N.I. and Schwartz, N.L. (1983) 'Conjectural variations', *Canadian Journal of Economics*, Vol. **XVI**, No. 2.

Krugman, P.R. (1979) 'Increasing returns, monopolistic competition and international trade', *Journal of International Economics*, **9**, pp. 469–79.

Layard, R. Nickell, S. and Jackman, R. (1984) 'European unemployment is Keynesian and classical but not structural', Centre for Labour Economics, LSE, Working Paper No. 862.

Neary, P. (1981) 'On the short-run effects of technological progress', *Oxford Economic Papers*, **33**, pp. 224–33.

Rosenberg, N. and Frischtak, C.R. (1984) 'Technological innovation and long waves', *Cambridge Journal of Economics*, **8**, pp. 1–24.

Salop, S. (1979) 'Monopolistic competition with outside goods', *Bell Journal of Economics*, **10**, pp. 141–56.

——and Perloff, J.M. (1985) 'Equilibrium with product differentiation', *Review of Economic Studies*, **L.II**, pp. 107–20.

Seade, J. (1980) 'On the effects of entry', *Econometrica*, **48**, pp. 479–89.

Shaked, A. and Sutton, J. (1982) 'Relaxing price competition through product differentiation', *Review of Economic Studies*, **49**, pp. 3–14.

——(1983a) 'Natural oligopolies', *Econometrica*, Vol. **51**, No. 5, pp. 1469–83.

——(1983b) 'Natural oligopolies and international trade' in Kierz-kowski, H. (Ed.) *Monopolistic Competition and International Trade* (1983), OUP, Oxford.

Sinclair, P.J.N. (1981) 'When will technical progress destroy jobs?', *Oxford Economic Papers*, **33**, pp. 1–18.

Solow, R. (1979a), 'Alternative approaches to macroeconomic theory: a partial view', *Canadian Journal of Economics*, Vol. **XII**, No. 3, pp. 339–54.

——(1979b) 'Another possible source of wage stickiness', *Journal of Macroeconomics*, Vol. **1**, No. 1, pp. 79–82.

——1980 'On theories of unemployment', *American Economic Review*, Vol. **70**, No. 1, pp. 1–11.

Standing, G. (1983) 'The notion of structural unemployment', *International Labour Review*, Vol. **22**, No. 2, pp. 137–53.

Stiglitz, J.E. (1984) 'Price rigidities and market structure', *American Economic Review*, pp. 350–5.

Stoneman, P., Blattner, N. and Pastre, O. (1982) 'Information technology, productivity and employment', in *Microelectronics, Robotics and Jobs*, ICCP, No. 7, OECD, Paris.

Stoneman, P. and Waterson, M. (1984) 'Employment, technological diffusion and oligopoly', mimeo, Warwick University.

Thornton, P. and Wheelock, V. (1980) 'Technology and employment: the prospects to 1990', *International Journal of Social Economics*, 1980–1, **7**, 1, pp. 24–36.

Varian, H.R. (1978) 'The stability of a disequilibrium IS–LM model' in *Topics in Disequilibrium Economics* Strom, S. and Werin, L. (Eds.), Macmillan, London.

Weitzman, M. (1982) 'Increasing returns and the foundations of unemployment theory', *Economic Journal*, **92**, pp. 787–804.

Wiles, P. (1983) 'Is Britain suffering from technological unemployment?', paper presented at Seminar on Unemployment, LSE Centre for Labour Economics.

Williams, B. (1983a) 'Technical change, employment and hours', paper presented at Seminar on Unemployment, LSE Centre for Labour Economics.

——(1983b) 'Technology's social consequences', *The Times Higher Educational Supplement* 12.8.83.

Wilson, R.A. and Whitley, J.D. (1982) 'Quantifying the employment effects of microelectronics', *Futures*, **14**, pp. 486–96.

Wragg, R. and Robertson, T. (1978) 'Post war trends in employment, productivity, output, labour costs and prices by industry in the UK', Research Paper No. 3, Department of Employment, London.

Index

SUBJECT INDEX

160

NAME INDEX